PIANO • VOCAL • CHORDS

Value Songbooks

CLASSIC ROCK

PLAY THE HITS *for less!*

Alfred Music Publishing Co., Inc.
16320 Roscoe Blvd., Suite 100
P.O. Box 10003
Van Nuys, CA 91410-0003
alfred.com

ISBN-10: 0-7390-6346-4
ISBN-13: 978-0-7390-6346-0

CONTENTS

Title	Artist	Page
19th Nervous Breakdown	The Rolling Stones	4
Another Brick in the Wall (Part 2)	Pink Floyd	10
Big Yellow Taxi	Joni Mitchell	30
Black Dog	Led Zeppelin	14
Black Water	The Doobie Brothers	20
Both Sides Now	Joni Mitchell	26
Can't Find My Way Home	Blind Faith	36
Casey Jones	Grateful Dead	44
Closer to the Heart	Rush	33
Comfortably Numb	Pink Floyd	54
Crazy Love	Van Morrison	50
Dear Mr. Fantasy	Traffic	62
Desperado	Eagles	68
Eight Miles High	The Byrds	59
Good Times, Bad Times	Led Zeppelin	74
Great Balls of Fire	Jerry Lee Lewis	80
Hot Fun in the Summertime	Sly and the Family Stone	85
Hotel California	Eagles	90
I Can See Clearly Now	Johnny Nash	98
Just What I Needed	The Cars	102
Layla	Derek and the Dominos	105
Let It Bleed	The Rolling Stones	112
Lights	Journey	119
Lola	The Kinks	124
Maggie May	Rod Stewart	130

Title	Artist	Page
Mama Told Me Not to Come	Three Dog Night	134
Margaritaville	Jimmy Buffett	140
Mustang Sally	Wilson Pickett	144
Piece of My Heart	Janis Joplin	148
Right Now	Van Halen	154
Roundabout	Yes	162
Running on Empty	Jackson Browne	178
She's a Rainbow	The Rolling Stones	186
Shower the People	James Taylor	192
Stairway to Heaven	Led Zeppelin	196
Sundown	Gordon Lightfoot	208
Sunshine of Your Love	Cream	212
Sympathy for the Devil	The Rolling Stones	216
Taxi	Harry Chapin	226
Time of the Season	Zombies	238
Tom Sawyer	Rush	252
The Trees	Rush	242
Uncle John's Band	Grateful Dead	259
Werewolves of London	Warren Zevon	266
Wheel in the Sky	Journey	278
Whipping Post	The Allman Brothers Band	284
White Room	Cream	290
Wild Horses	The Rolling Stones	273
Wish You Were Here	Pink Floyd	300
You Can Leave Your Hat On	Joe Cocker	294

19TH NERVOUS BREAKDOWN

Words and Music by
MICK JAGGER and KEITH RICHARDS

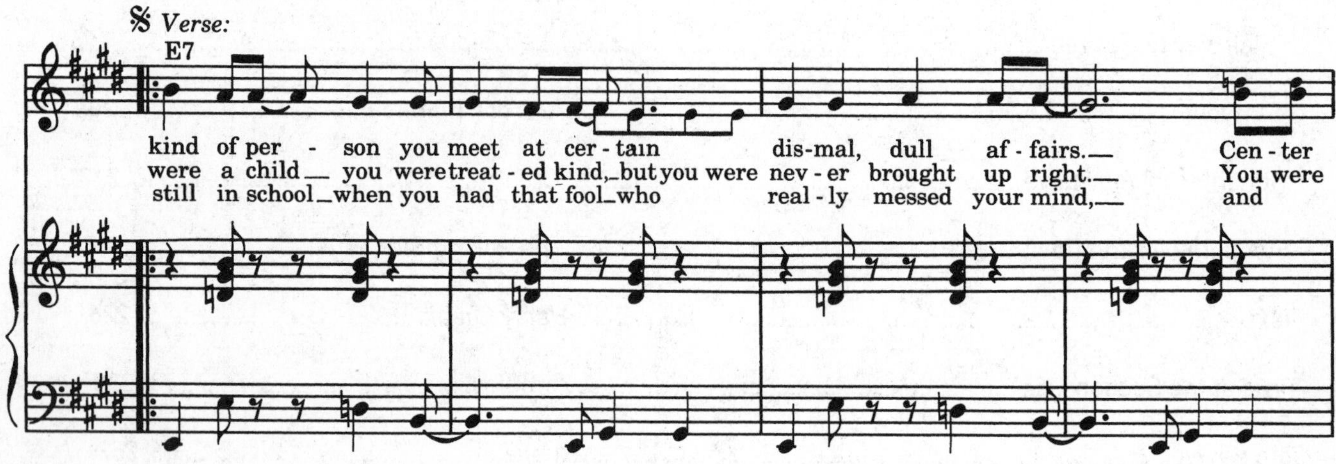

A
seems to me that you have seen too much in too few years, and
mother who neglected you owes a million dollars tax, and your
our first trip I tried so hard to re-arrange your mind, but
E7
though you've tried, you just can't hide your eyes are edged with tears.
father's still perfecting ways of making ceiling wax.
after a while I realized you were disarranging mine.
You better
To Coda
Bsus 2 4
B
Bsus 2 4
B
N.C.
stop,
look around.
Here it

Chorus:
E7
comes, ___
here it
E
comes, ___
here it
A
A7
comes, ___
A6
A
here it
comes. ___
A7
A6
A
Here
E7
comes your nine - teenth
ner-vous break-down. ___
1.

2.
To Next Strain
E7
2. When you
3.
E7
N.C.
Esus$\frac{2}{4}$ E
Esus$\frac{2}{4}$ E
Esus$\frac{2}{4}$ E
Esus$\frac{2}{4}$ E

B
Oh, who's to blame, that
E7
girl's just in - sane. Well,
A/E Asus 2/4/E A/E Asus 2/4/E A/E B/E Bsus 2/4/E B/E Bsus 2/4/E B/E
nothing I do don't seem to work, it only seems to make matters worse. Oh,

E7
1.
D. S. 𝄋
please.
3. You were
2.
E7
D. S. 𝄋 al Coda
2. When you
Coda
N. C.
round,
E7
here it comes.
Here
Repeat and Fade
comes your nine - teenth nervous break - down.
Here

ANOTHER BRICK IN THE WALL (PART 2)

Words and Music by
ROGER WATERS

Teach - er, leave_ them
Teach - ers, leave_ them
G
3
kids a - lone._
kids a - lone._
Hey!
Hey!
Dm
Dm
10
C
8
Teach-er!
Teach-er!
Leave them kids a - lone!___
Leave us kids a - lone!___
Dm
10
C
8
G
7
F
5
F
All in all, it's just an -
All in all, you're just an -

C
Dm
oth - er brick in the wall.
oth - er brick in the wall.
F
C
1.
Dm
N.C.
All in all, it's just an - oth - er brick in the wall.
All in all, you're just an - oth - er brick in the
(Drums)
2.
Dm
wall.
C
Dm
C
(Inst. solo ad lib. to end)

Dm
C
Dm
C/D
Dm
C/D
Dm
G/D
Dm7
G/D
Dm
C/D
B♭/D
C/D
Dm
N.C.
(Drums & dialogue fade to end)

BLACK DOG

Words and Music by
JIMMY PAGE, ROBERT PLANT
and JOHN PAUL JONES

Blues rock ♩= 168
Verses 1 & 3:
A5
*
1. Hey, hey, ma - ma, said the way you move,_ gon - na make you sweat,_ gon - na
3. See additional lyrics
tacet 1st time
mf

N.C.
make you groove.___
3

A5
Ah - ah, child,_ way you shake that thing,_ gon - na

* Vocal sung 1 octave higher.

N.C.
make you burn, gon - na make you sting.
A5
Hey, hey, ba - by, when you
walk that way, watch your hon - ey drip, can't keep a - way.
N.C.

A5
Oh
Chorus:
C5
A5
yeah,
oh
yeah,
ah
ah
ah.
Oh

C5
A5
yeah, oh yeah, ah ah ah.
Verses 2 & 4:
2. I got - ta roll, can't stand still, got a flam - ing heart, can't
4. See additional lyrics
N.C.
A5
get my fill.
cue notes 2nd time only
Eyes that shine, burn - ing red, dreams of you all

N.C.
through my head.
A5
Ah ah ah ah ah ah
N.C.
To Coda
A
ah ah ah ah ah ah ah. Hey
Bridge:
C
A
G/E
ba - by, oh ba - by, pret - ty ba - by,
dar - ling,
move me

Verse 3:
Didn't take too long before I found out what
People mean by "down and out."

Spent my money, took my car,
Started telling her friends she gonna be a star.

I don't know, but I been told,
A big-legged woman ain't got no soul.
(To Chorus:)

Verse 4:
All I ask for, all I pray,
Steady-rolling woman gonna come my way.

Need a woman gonna hold my hand,
Will tell me no lies, make me a happy man.
Ah ah ah ah ah ah ah ah ah ah ah ah ah.
(To Coda)

BLACK WATER

Words and Music by
PATRICK SIMMONS

Am7
D
Cat - fish are jump-in', that pad - dle wheel thump - in', black
wa - ter keeps roll - in' on past just the same.
G
Bb
Old black wa - ter, keep on roll - in',
Mis - sis-sip-pi moon, won't you
keep on shin - in' on me?
Old black wa - ter, keep on roll - in',
Mis -

Bb
G
Old black wa - ter,
sis-sip-pi moon, won't you keep on shin - in' on me?
keep on roll - in',
Bb
Mis - sis-sip-pi moon, won't you keep on shin - in' on
A
Em7
A
Em7
me? Yeah, keep on shin - in' your light, gon-na make
A
Em7
A
Em7
ev - 'ry - thing, pret-ty ma-ma, gon-na make ev - 'ry-thing all right.

D
Am7
And I ain't got no wor - ries 'cause I
D
Am7
A
Em7
ain't in no hur - ry at all.
A
Am7
D
Am7
To Coda
D
Am7
D
Well, if it rains, I don't care, don't make no

Am7
D
Am7
dif - fer - ence to me; just take that street - car that's go -
D
Am7
D
Am7
in' up - town.
Yeah, I'd like to hear some fun - ky
D
Am7
D
Dix - ie - land and dance a hon - ky - tonk, and I'll be
Am7
D
Am7
D
D. S. al Coda
buy-in' ev-'ry-bod-y drinks all 'roun'.

Coda
Repeat and fade
D
Am7
D
I'd like to hear some fun - ky Dix. - ie - land, pret-ty ma -
Am7
D
Am7
ma, come and take me by the hand, by the hand. Take me by the
I want to hon-ky-tonk, hon-ky -
D
Am7
D
hand, pret-ty ma-ma, come and dance with your dad-dy all night long. I'd like to
tonk, hon-ky-tonk with you all night long.

Gtr. tuned to "Open E":
E-7-5-4-3-5
⑥ = E ③ = G♯
⑤ = B ② = B
④ = E ① = E

BOTH SIDES NOW

Words and Music by
JONI MITCHELL

Moderately ♩ = 98

Guitar Capo 2 → *E* *A(9)* *E* *A(9)* *E* *A(9)* *E* *A(9)* *E*
Piano → F♯ B(9) F♯ B(9) F♯ B(9) F♯ B(9) F♯

mp *legato*

Verse:

Emaj7 *A(9)* *E* *B7* *E* *A(9)* *E* *B7sus* *B7*
F♯maj7 B(9) F♯ C♯7 F♯ B(9) F♯ C♯7sus C♯7

1. Bows and flows of an - gel hair and ice - cream cas - tles
2. Moons and Junes and Fer - ris wheels, the diz - zy danc - ing
3. *See additional lyrics*

E *B7* *E* *Emaj7* *A(9)* *B7sus* *E*
F♯ C♯7 F♯ F♯maj7 B(9) C♯7sus F♯

in the air, and feath-er can - yons ev-'ry-where,
way you feel, as ev - 'ry fair - y tale comes real,

Emaj7
A(9)
E
B7sus
F♯maj7
B(9)
F♯
C♯7sus
E
Emaj7
A(9)
F♯
F♯maj7
B(9)
I've looked at clouds that way.
I've looked at love that way.
But now they on - ly
But now it's just an -
B7sus
E
A(9)
E
B7sus
B7
E
B7
C♯7sus
F♯
B(9)
F♯
C♯7sus
C♯7
F♯
C♯7
block the sun, they rain and snow on ev - 'ry - one. So
oth - er show, you leave 'em laugh - ing when you go. And
Emaj7
A(9)
B7sus
E
F♯maj7
B(9)
C♯7sus
F♯
man - y things I would have done,
if you care, don't let them know,
Emaj7
A(9)
E
B7sus
F♯maj7
B(9)
F♯
C♯7sus
but clouds got in my way.
don't give your - self a - way.

Chorus:
E
B7
Emaj7
A(9)
B7sus
F♯
C♯7
F♯maj7
B(9)
C♯7sus
I've looked at clouds from both sides now, from up and down, and
I've looked at love from both sides now, from give and take, and
3.4. See additional lyrics
still some - how, it's cloud il - lu - sions I re - call, I
still some - how, it's love's il - lu - sions I re - call, I
real - ly don't know clouds
real - ly don't know love

Verse 3:
Tears and fears and feeling proud,
To say "I Love You," right out loud
Dreams and schemes and circus crowds
I've looked at life that way
But now old friends are acting strange
They shake their heads, they say I've changed
Well, something's lost, but something's gained
In living every day.

Chorus 3:
I've looked at life from both sides now
From win and lose, and still somehow
It's life's illusions I recall
I really don't know life at all.

Chorus 4:
I've looked at life from both sides now
From up and down, and still somehow
It's life's illusions I recall
I really don't know life at all.

BIG YELLOW TAXI

Words and Music by
JONI MITCHELL

F F6 F7 B♭ E♭ C
with a pink ho - tel, a bou-tique, and a
and they charged all the peo-ple a dol - lar and a half just to
Give me spots on my ap-ples, but leave me the birds and the
and a big yel - low tax - i took a - way my old
F F6 F7 F6 F F6
swing - ing hot spot.
see 'em.
bees, please!
man.
Chorus:
F F7
Don't it al - ways seem to go that you don't know what you've got
B♭ E♭ C
till it's gone? They paved par - a - dise and put up a park - ing lot.

1.2.3.
F
F6
F7
F6
F
F6
F
F6
F
F6
F7
F6
(Woo, bop bop bop bop.) Woo, bop
bop bop bop.)
4.
F
F6
F
F6
F
F6
F7
F6
F
F6
F
F6
2. They
(Woo, bop bop bop bop.)
Chorus:
F
F7
Don't it al - ways seem to go that you don't know what you've got till it's gone? They
Repeat ad lib. and fade
B♭
E♭
C
F
F6
F7
F6
F
F6
F
F6
paved par - a - dise and put up a park - ing lot. They
a tempo

CLOSER TO THE HEART

Words by
NEIL PEART and PETER TALBOT

Music by
GEDDY LEE and ALEX LIFESON

Verse:
A
G
D
G
A
men who hold_ high plac - es must be the ones_ who start___ to
2.3.4. See additional lyrics
f
G
D
A
G
mold a new__ re-al-i-ty clos - er to___ the heart,___
1.
D
A
G
clos - er to___ the heart.___ 2. The
2.
D
A
G
clos - er to___ the heart.___
D
3. Phi -
mf

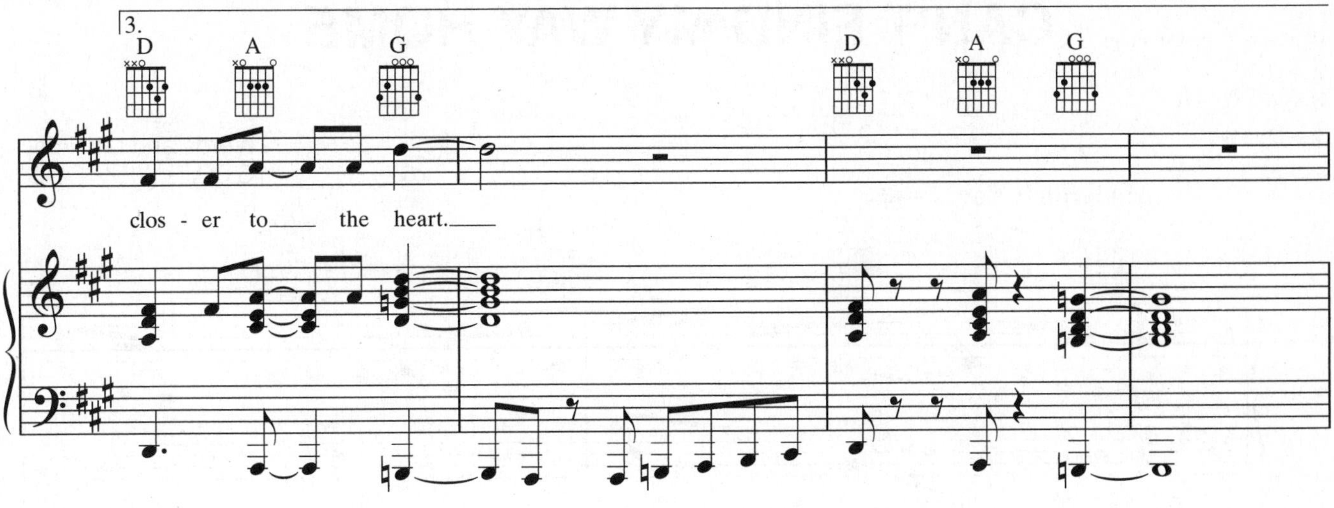

3.

D A G D A G

clos - er to___ the heart.___

A(add B)

mf

Verse 2:
The blacksmith and the artist
Reflect it in their art.
They forge their creativity
Closer to the heart,
Closer to the heart.
(To Verse 3:)

Verse 3:
Philosophers and ploughmen,
Each must know his part
To sow a new mentality
Closer to the heart,
Closer to the heart.
(To Verse 4:)

Verse 4:
You can be the captain;
I will draw the chart,
Sailing into destiny
Closer to the heart,
Closer to the heart.

CAN'T FIND MY WAY HOME

All gtrs. in Drop D tuning:
⑥ = D ③ = G
⑤ = A ② = B
④ = D ① = E

Words and Music by
STEVE WINWOOD

F
G
D
Some - bod - y must change.
C2
G/B
Gm/B♭
D/A
You are the rea - son I've been wait - ing so long.
F
G
D
Some - bod - y holds the key. Well, I'm
Chorus 1:
G/B
Asus
A
near the end, I just ain't got the time,

D
Em
and I'm wast - ed and I
G
F♯m
Em
D
can't find my way home.
C2
G/B
Gm/B♭
D/A
F
G
D
C2
G/B
Gm/B♭
D/A
Ooh.

F G D

Ooh.________ 2. Come

Verse 2:

C2 G/B Gm/B♭ D/A

down on__ your own________ and leave your bod-y a-lone.________

F G D

Some - bod - y__ must change._

C2 G/B Gm/B♭ D/A

You are__ the rea - son I've been wait-ing all__ these____ years.______

F
G
D
Some - bod - y holds the key.
Well, I'm
Chorus 2:
G/B
Asus
A
near the end, I just ain't got the time,
D
Em
oh, and I'm wast - ed and I
G
F♯m
Em
D
can't find my way home.

Interlude:

C2
G/B
Gm/B♭
D/A
F
G
D
C2
G/B
Ooh,
Gm/B♭
D/A
F
G
but I can't find my way
D
C2
G/B
Gm/B♭
D/A
home.
Ah,
but I

F
G
D
can't find my way home.
Ooh,
C2
G/B
Gm/B♭
D/A
but I can't
F
G
D
find my way home.
Ah,
C2
G/B
Gm/B♭
D/A
dee, doo,
but I

F
G
D
can't find my way home.
Still I can't
find my way home.
And I
ain't done nothing wrong,
but I
can't find my way home.
poco rit.

CASEY JONES

Words by
ROBERT HUNTER

Music by
JERRY GARCIA

Medium beat

mf

C F(add G) Fsus4

Driv - ing that train,__ high on co - caine,__

F Fsus4 F C

Ca - sey Jones,_ you'd bet - ter watch your speed._

F(add G) Fsus4

Trou - ble a - head,__ trou - ble be - hind,__

F
Fsus 4
F
C
C
F
and you know that no-tion just crossed my_ mind. _
C
C
D
This old en - gine makes it on time, _
Trou-ble with you_ is the trou - ble with me; _ got
F
G
C
leaves Cen-tral Sta - tion 'bout a quar-ter to nine. _ Hits Riv-er Junc - tion at
two good eyes_ but we still _ don't see. _ Come round the bend, _ you
D
F
E7
Am
G7
sev-en-teen to; _ at a quar - ter to ten _ you know it's trav-'lin' a-gain. _
know it's the end. _ The fire - man screams- and the en-gine just gleams. _

C
F
Driv - ing that train,
high on co - caine,
C
Ca - sey Jones, you'd bet - ter
watch your speed.
F
Trou - ble a - head,
trou - ble be - hind,
C
To Coda
and you know that no - tion
just crossed my mind.

C F C

C A+ D F

Trou-ble a-head, the la-dy in red, take my ad-vice, you'd be

G C

bet-ter off dead. Switch-man's sleep-ing, Train

D F E7 Am G7

Hun-dred and Two is on the wrong track and head-ed for you.

Chorus
C
F
Driv - ing that train,
high on co - caine,
C
Ca - sey Jones, you'd bet - ter
watch your speed.
F
Trou - ble a - head,
trou - ble be - hind,
C
D. S. al Coda
and you know that no - tion
just crossed my mind.

Coda

C Bb F

Driv - ing that train, ___ high ___ on co - caine, ___ Ca -

C

sey Jones, you'd bet - ter watch your speed. ___ Trou - ble a - head, ___ trou -

Bb F

1. 2. 3. C

ble be - hind, ___ and ___ you know that no - tion just crossed my ___ mind.

4. C A7 D7 G7 C

just crossed my mind. ___ And you know that no - tion just crossed my mind. ___

rit.

CRAZY LOVE

Words and Music by
VAN MORRISON

Slowly ♩ = 72
Verses 1 & 2:
A
C♯m
D
A
1. I can hear her heart-beat for a thou - sand miles, and the
fine sense of hu - mor when I'm feel - in' low down. And when
mp
(with pedal)

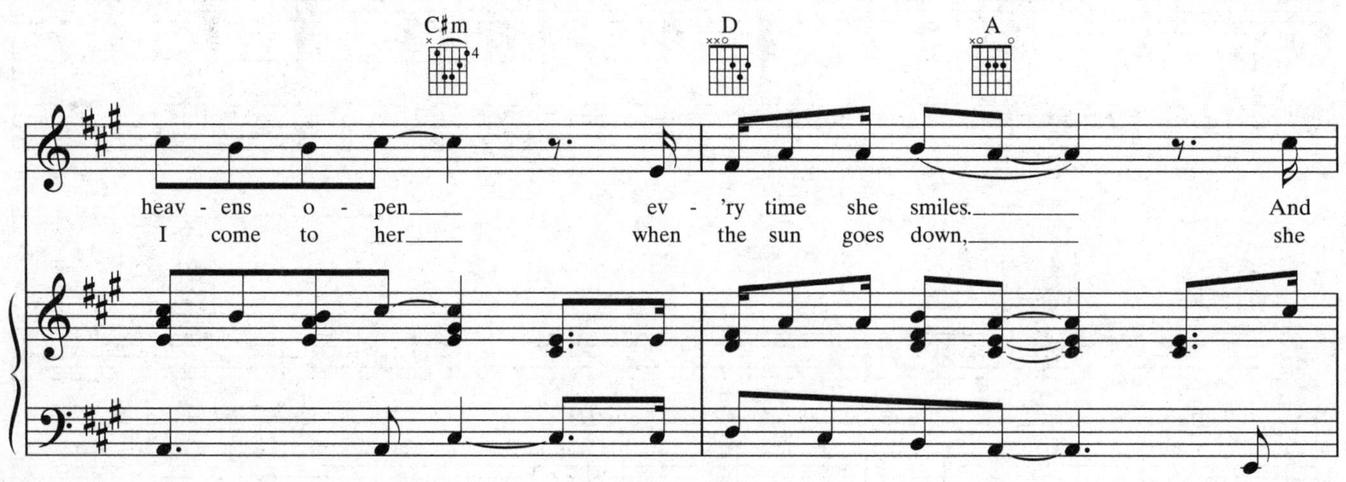
C♯m
D
A
heav - ens o - pen ev - 'ry time she smiles. And
I come to her when the sun goes down, she

C♯m
D
A
when I come to her, that's where I be - long. Yes, I'm
takes a - way my trou - ble, takes a-way my grief. Takes a -

C♯m
D
A
run - ning to her like a riv - er's song.
way my heart - ache in the night like a thief.
She gives me
Chorus:
E/G♯
F♯m
F♯m/E
D
E
A
E/G♯
F♯m
F♯m/E
love, love, love, love, cra - zy love.
She gives me love, love, love, love,
1.
2.
Bridge:
D
A
D
A
E
D
cra - zy love.
2. She's got a cra - zy love.
And I need her in the
A
E
D
A
day - time,
and I need her in the night.

E
D
A
F♯m
And I want to throw my arms a-round her and
Bm7
E
A
E
kiss her, hug her, kiss her, hug her tight.
3. And when
Verse 3:
A
C♯m
D
A
I'm re-turn-ing from so far a-way, she gives me
C♯m
D
A
such sweet lov-in', bright-ens up my day.
Yeah, it

A
C♯m
D
A
makes me right - eous
and it makes me whole.
C♯m
D
A
And it makes me mel - low
down to my soul.
She gives me
Chorus:
E/G♯
F♯m
F♯m/E
D
E
A
E/G♯
F♯m
F♯m/E
love, love, love, love,
cra - zy love.
She gives me
love, love, love, love,
1.
D
A
2.
D
A
cra - zy love.
She's got a
cra - zy love.

COMFORTABLY NUMB

Words and Music by
ROGER WATERS and DAVID GILMOUR

Slowly ♩ = 66
Bm
mp

Verse:
A
1. Hel - lo, (Hel - lo, hel - lo.___) is there an - y - bod - y in there? Just nod if you can

G
Em
Bm
hear me. Is there an - y - one___ home?

A
Come on, now, I hear you're feel - ing down. Well,
(Come on, come on.)
2. O - kay, (O - kay, o - kay.) just a lit - tle pin - prick. There'll be no more...
G
Em7
Bm
I can ease your pain, get you on your feet a - gain.
("ah,") but you may feel a lit - tle sick. Can you
Bm
A
Re - lax, (Re - lax, re - lax.) I need some in - for - ma - tion first.
stand up? (Stand up, stand up.) I do be - lieve it's work - ing. Good. That-'ll keep you

G
Em7
Bm
Just the ba - sic facts, can you show me where it hurts?
go - ing for the show. Come on, it's time to go.
Chorus:
D
A
There is no pain, you are re - ced - ing.
mf
D
A
G/B
A dis - tant ship's smoke on the ho - ri - zon.
C
G
You are on - ly com - ing through in waves. Your
sim.

C G

lips move,__ but I can't hear__ what you're say - ing.

1. When
3. When

D A

I was a child, I had__ a fe - ver. My

2. *(Gtr. solo ad lib….*
I was a child, I caught__ a fleet - ing glimpse,__

D A G/B

hands felt__ just like__ two__ bal - loons.__

out__ of the cor - ner of my eye.__

C G

Now I've got__ that feel - ing once__ a - gain.__ I__ can't ex - plain, you would not un -

I turned__ to look,__ but it__ was gone,__ I can - not put__ my fin - ger on__

C
G
der - stand,_ this is not how_ I am._
_ it now._ The child is grown,_ the dream_ is gone._
...end solo)
A
G/B
C
G
I_ have be - come_ com - f'rta - bly
1.
2.
D.S. 𝄋
3.
D
numb.
numb.
numb.
cresc.
Repeat ad lib. and fade
Bm
A
G
Em
Bm
(Gtr. solo ad lib.)

EIGHT MILES HIGH

Words and Music by
GENE CLARK, DAVID CROSBY
and JIM McGUINN

Moderately ♩ = 128

N.C.

mf

Em

Guitar solo ad lib.

𝄋 *Verse:*

Em F♯m7 G D C

1. Eight miles high and when you touch down
2. No - where is there warmth to be found
3. 'Round the squares, hud - dled in storms,

3

G D C(9) C C(9)
you'll find that it's strang - er than known.
a - mong those a - fraid of los - ing their ground.
some laugh - ing, some just shape - less forms.
Em F♯m7 G D C
Signs in the street that say where you're go - ing
Rain - gray town known for its sound,
Side - walk scenes and black lim - ou - sines,
To Coda
G D C C(9)
1.
are some - where just be - ing their own.
in plac - es small fac - es un - bound.
some liv - ing, some stand - ing a - lone.
Em F♯m7 G F♯m7
2.

Em
Play six times, Guitar solo ad lib.
D.S. 𝄋 al Coda
𝄌 Coda
Em
F♯m7
Em
F♯m7
Guitar solo, repeat as desired
Em
F♯m7
Em
F♯m7
Em

DEAR MR. FANTASY

Words and Music by
STEVE WINWOOD,
CHRIS WOOD and JIM CAPALDI

D A

some - thing to make_ us all__ hap - py.________

G

Do an - y - thing,__ take__ us out of this__ gloom.________ Sing a song,_

D A

__ play gui - tar,___ make it snap - py.______

G

You are the one___ who__ can make us all__ laugh,_____ but

D
A
doing that, you break out in tears.
G
Please don't be sad if it was a straight mind you had, we
D
A
To Coda
would-n't have known you all these years.
F♯m
A
F♯m
Ooh, ah. Ooh,

A
F♯m
A
ah.
Ooh,
ah.
F♯m
G
E7
Ohh,
ah,
ah.
Verse 2:
A
G
2. Dear Mis - ter Fan - ta - sy, play us a tune,
D
A
some - thing to make us all hap - py.

G
Do an - y - thing, take us out of this gloom. Sing a song,
D
A
play gui - tar, make it snap - py, yeah, yeah.
Instrumental solo ad lib.:
A
G
D
f
A
Play 7 times
G
D
A
D.S. 𝄋 al Coda

Coda
Instrumental solo ad lib.:
G
D
A
A5
Play 5 times
Repeat and fade

DESPERADO

Words and Music by
DON HENLEY and GLENN FREY

G
G7
C
Cm6
hard one, I know that you got your rea - sons, these
G/D
G+/D♯
Em
A7
D7
G
D/F♯
things that are pleas - in' you can hurt you some - how. Don't you
cresc.
Em
Bm7
C
G
draw the queen of dia - monds, boy, she'll beat you if she's a - ble. You know the
mf
Em
C
G
D/F♯
queen of hearts is al - ways your best bet. Now it

Em7
Bm7
C
G
seems to me some fine things have been laid up-on your ta-ble, but you
Em
A7
Am7/D
D
on-ly want the ones that you can't get. Des-per-a-
poco rit. decresc.
G
G7
C
G/B
Am7
do, oh, you ain't get-tin' no young-er, your
a tempo
G
D/F♯
Em
A7
D7
pain and your hun-ger, they're driv-in' you home. And
3

G
G7
C
G/B
Am7
free-dom, oh, free-dom, well, that's just some peo-ple talk - in'. Your
G/D
G+/D♯
Em
A7
D7
G
D/F♯
3
pris - on is walk - in' through this world all a - lone. Don't your
cresc.
Em
Bm7
C
G
feet get cold in the win-ter-time? The sky won't snow and the sun won't shine. It's
mf
Em
C
G
D
hard to tell the night-time from the day. You're

Em7
Bm7
C
G
los - in' all your highs and lows. Ain't it fun - ny how the feel - ing goes
Am7
C/D
D
G
G7
a - way? Des - per - a - do, why don't you
C
Cm6
G
D/F♯
Em
come to your sens - es? Come down from your fenc - es,
A7
D7
G
G7
o - pen the gate. It may be rain - in', but there's a

C
C6
G
D/F♯
Em
rain-bow a - bove_ you. You bet-ter let some - bod - y love you,
C
G/B
Am7
Am7/D
G/D
G+/D♯
Em
you___ bet-ter let some - bod - y love___ you_______ be -
Am7/D
G
G7
fore it's too_______ late.
mp
a tempo
C
Cm6
G(9)
rit.

GOOD TIMES BAD TIMES

Words and Music by
JIMMY PAGE, JOHN PAUL JONES
and JOHN BONHAM

Moderate rock ♩ = 96

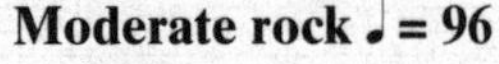

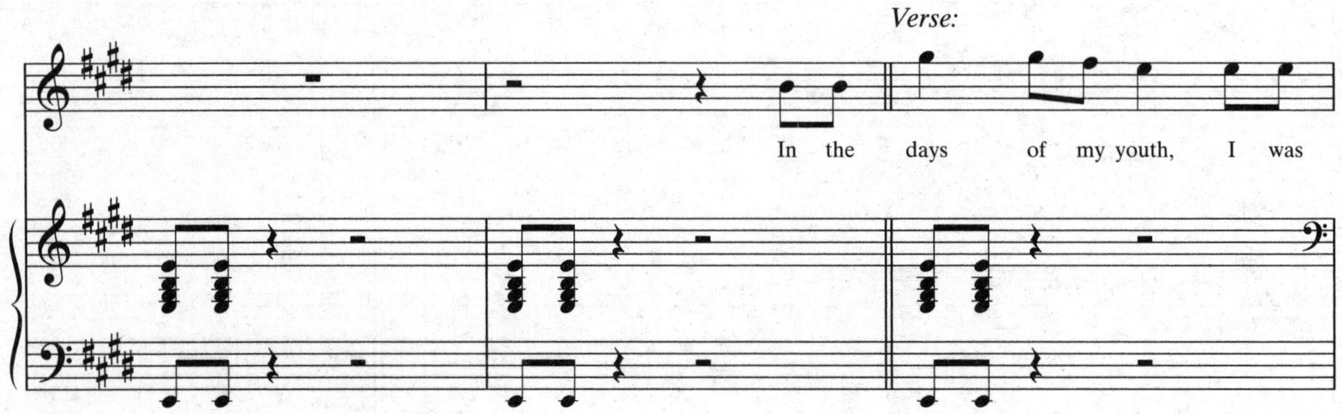

D
A
E
And now I've reached that age, I've tried to do
all those things the best I can.
No mat - ter how I try, I find my
way in - to the same old jam.

Chorus:
A
G
D
A
G
D
Good times, bad times, you know I've had my share. Well, my
B
A
E
B
wom-an left home for a brown-eyed man, but I still don't seem to care.
Bridge:
F♯5
N.C.
Six - teen, I fell in love with a
girl as sweet as could be. It on - ly took a cou - ple of days till

she was rid of me.
She swore that she would be all mine and
love me till the end,
but when I whis-pered in her ear, I
Chorus:
B
A/E
E
lost an-oth-er friend, oh!
Good times, bad times, you
B
A/E
E
C#
B
F#
know I've had my share.
Well, my wom-an left home for a brown-eyed man, but I

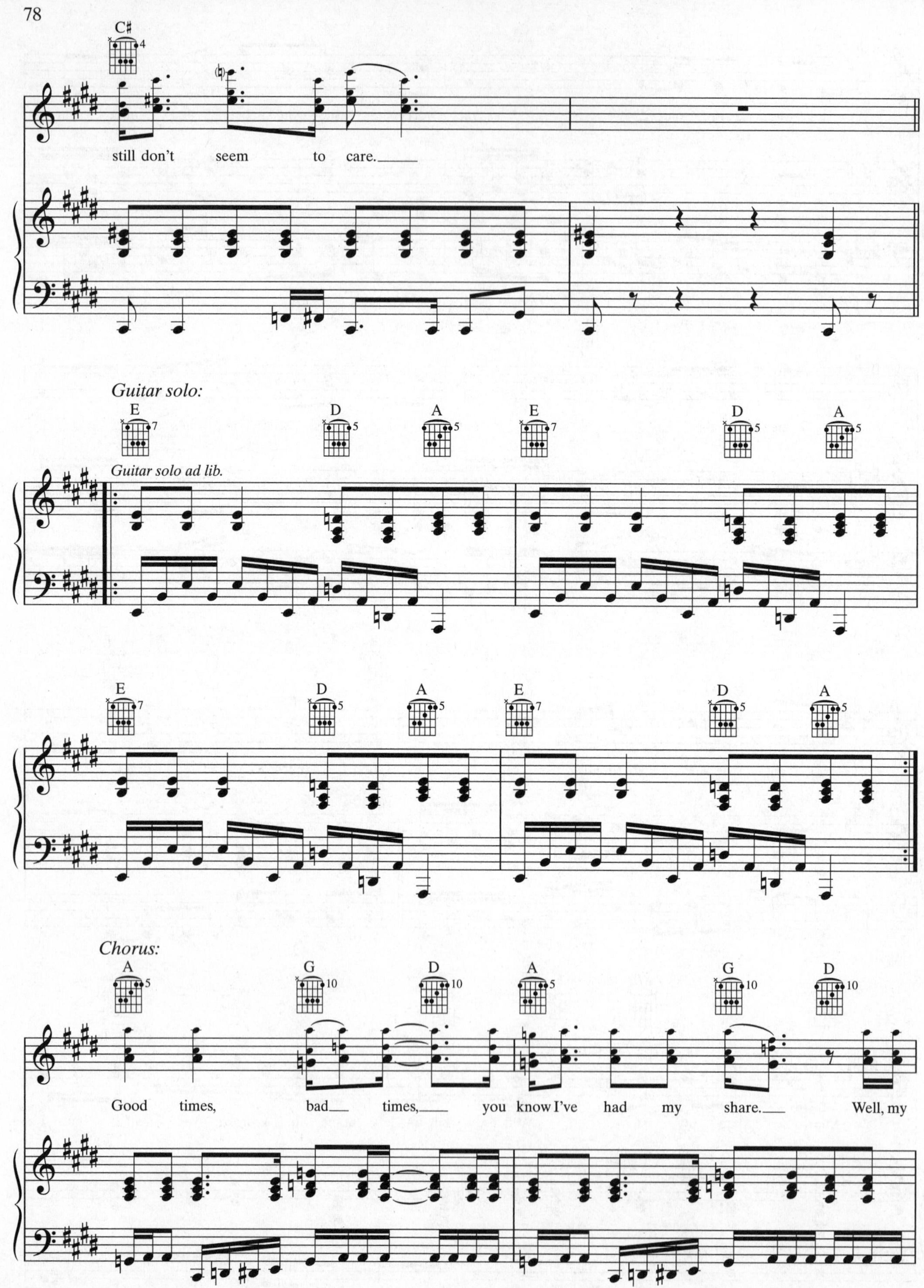
C♯
still don't seem to care.
Guitar solo:
E
D
A
Guitar solo ad lib.
Chorus:
A
G
D
Good times, bad times, you know I've had my share. Well, my

Ad lib. vocal:
I know what it means to be alone,
I sure do wish I was at home.
I don't care what the neighbors say,
I'm gonna love you each and every day.
You can feel the beat within my heart.
Realize, sweet babe, we ain't never gonna part.

GREAT BALLS OF FIRE

Words and Music by
OTIS BLACKWELL and JACK HAMMER

Rock and roll ♩ = 152

I laughed at love 'cause I thought it was fun - ny.
8va
Gliss.
F7
G7
You came a - long and you moved me, hon - ey. I changed my mind,
F7
C
N.C.
this love is fine. Good - ness gra - cious, great balls of fire!
F7
C
Kiss me, ba - by. Hmm, it feels

F7
good. Hold me, ba - by. Well,
8va
Gliss.
G7
I want to love you like a lov - er should. You're fine,
so kind. Got to tell this world that you're mine, mine, mine, mine.
C
F7
I chew my nails and I twid - dle my thumbs. I'm real ner-vous, but it
Gliss.

To Coda
G7
F7
sure is fun.
C - 'mon, ba - by, you're driv - ing me cra - zy.
C7
N.C.
Piano solo:
C
Good - ness gra - cious, great balls of fire!
F7
8va
Glissando
Gliss.
G7
F7
C
(8va)
Gliss.
Gliss.

(8va)
F7
G7
(8va)
F7
C
D.S. 𝄋 al Coda
Well!
(8va)
Glissando
𝄌 Coda
C7
N.C.
C
Good - ness gra - cious, great balls of fire!

HOT FUN IN THE SUMMERTIME

Words and Music by
SYLVESTER STEWART

E♭
hi there. Them
Dm7
G7
sum - mer days,
those sum - mer days.
Dm7
C/E
F
Am
G7
Dm7/G
C/G
F/G
Verses 2 & 3:
C
Gm9
2. That's when I had most of my fun
3. First of the fall and there she goes

Dm7(♭5)
A♭(9)
Gm7
Fm7(4)
back.
back.
Hi,
Bye,
hi,
bye,
hi,
bye,
E♭
hi
bye
there.
there.
Them
Them
Dm7
G7
sum - mer days,
sum - mer days,
those sum - mer days.
those sum - mer days.
Dm7
C/E
F
Am
G
N.C.
I cloud nine when I want
Ba ba ba ba ba when I

Dm7
C/E
F
Am
G7
N.C.
want to.
to.
Out of school,
count-y fair in the coun-
try sun,
and ev-'ry-thing is
cool,
ooh, yeah.
F♯m7(♭5)
G
G/G♯
G/A
Em7(4)
To Coda

Chorus:

Dm7 C/E F Am G7 Dm7 C/E F Am G7

Hot fun in the sum - mer - time.__ Hot fun in the

Dm7 C/E F Am G7

sum - mer - time.__ Hot fun in the sum - mer - time.__

Dm7 C/E F F♯m7(♭5) G7

D.S. 𝄋 al Coda

Hot fun in the sum - mer - time.__

𝄌 Coda

Dm7 C/E F Am G7

Repeat and fade

Hot fun in the sum - mer - time.__

HOTEL CALIFORNIA

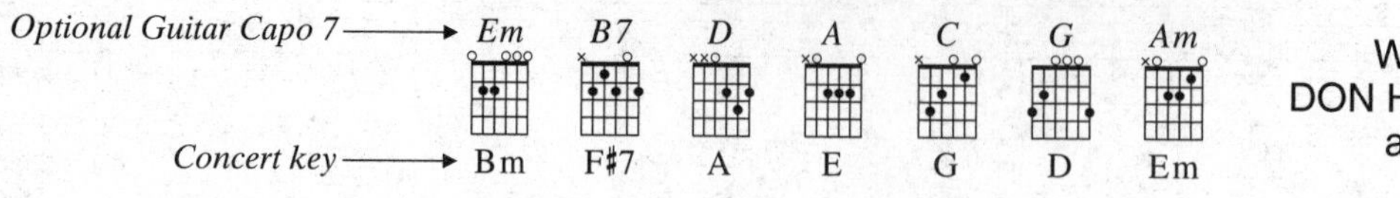

Words and Music by
DON HENLEY, GLENN FREY
and DON FELDER

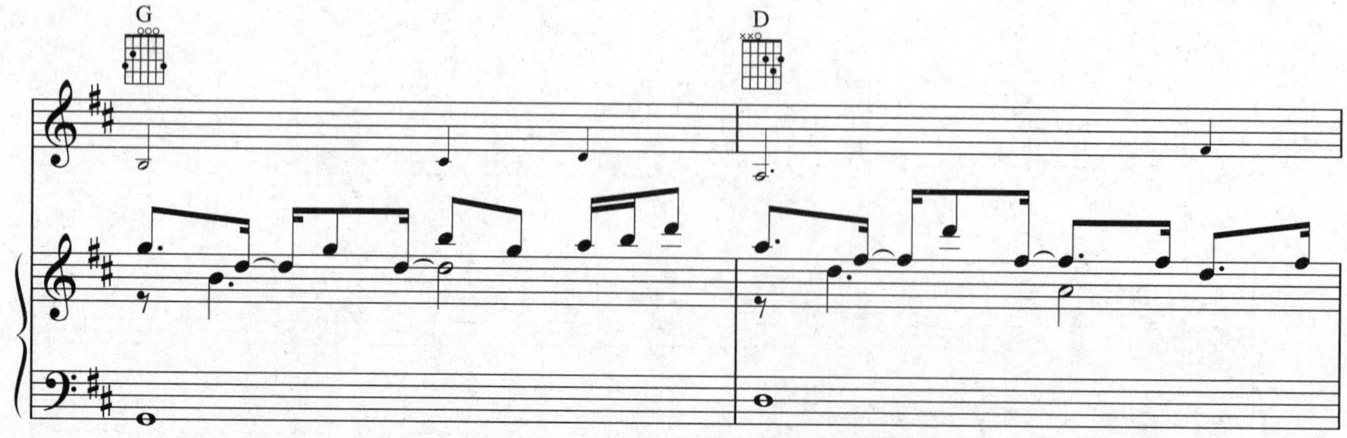

Em
1.
F♯7
2.
F♯7
Verses 1 & 2:
Bm
F♯7
mf
1. On a dark des-ert high-way, cool wind in my hair,
2. Her mind is Tif - fa - ny twist - ed, she got the Mer - ce - des bends.
A
E
warm smell of co-li - tas ris - ing up through the air.
She got a lot of pret-ty, pret-ty boys that she calls friends.
G
D
Up a - head in the dis - tance, I saw a shim-mer-ing light.
How they dance in the court - yard, sweet sum-mer sweat.

Em
F#7
My head grew heav - y and my sight grew dim,
I had to stop for the night.
Some dance to re-mem - ber,
some dance to for - get.
Bm
F#7
There she stood in the door - way,
I heard the mis - sion bell.
So I called up the cap - tain,
"Please bring me my wine."
He said,
A
E
And I was think - ing to my - self, "This could be heav - en or this could be hell."
"We have - n't had that spir - it here since nine - teen six - ty - nine.
G
D
Then she lit up a can - dle and she showed me the way.
And still those voic - es are call - ing from far a - way,

Em F♯7

There were voic - es down the cor - ri - dor,_ I thought I heard them say,_
wake you up in the mid - dle of the night just to hear them say,_

Chorus:

G D

"Wel - come_ to the Ho - tel Cal - i - for - nia! Such a

F♯7 Bm

love - ly place,_ (such a love - ly place,_) such a love - ly face._ They're

G D

Plen - ty of room_ at the Ho - tel Cal - i - for - nia, an - y
liv - in' it up__ at the Ho - tel Cal - i - for - nia. What a

Em
1.
F#7
time_ of year_ (an - y time_ of year_) you can find_ it here._
nice_ sur - prise,_ (what a nice_ sur - prise,_) bring your
2.
F#7
N.C.
Verse 3:
Bm
al - i - bis.__
Mir - rors__ on the ceil - ing,____
mp
F#7
A
the pink cham - pagne on ice,__ and she said,
"We are all just pris - on - ers here_
E
G
of our own_ de - vice."
And in the mas - ter's_ cham - bers,____

D Em

they gath-ered for the feast. They stab it__ with their steel-y knives,_ but they

F♯7 Bm

just can't__ kill the beast. Last thing_ I re-mem-ber, I was

F♯7 A

run-ning_ for the door. I had to find the pas-sage back_ to the

E G

place I was_ be-fore.____ "Re-lax," said the night-man. *"We are_*

D
Em
pro - grammed_ to re - ceive.
You can check out an - y - time you like,
F♯7
N.C.
Solo:
Bm
but you can_ nev - er leave."_
(Inst. solo ad lib....
(Cue notes 2nd time only)
F♯7
A
E
G
D
Em

1.2.
F♯7
3.
F♯7
…end solo)
Bm
F♯7
A
E
G
D
Em
F♯7
Repeat and fade

I CAN SEE CLEARLY NOW

Words and Music by
JOHNNY NASH

Reggae ♩ = 120

N.C.
(Percussion)
mp

Verse:
D
G
D
1. I can see clear - ly now, the rain is gone.
2. Oh yes, I can make it now, the pain is gone.
3. I can see clear - ly now, the rain is gone.
mf

G
I can see all ob - sta - cles
All of the bad feel - ings have
I can see all ob - sta - cles

A
D
in my way.
dis - ap - peared.
in my way.
Gone are the dark
Here is that rain -
Here is that rain -
G
D
clouds that had me down.
bow I've been pray - ing for.
bow I've been pray - ing for.
It's gon-na be a bright,
C
G
D
To Coda
bright, sun-shin - y day.
(bright, bright,)
1.
C
G
It's gon-na be a bright, bright, sun-shin - y day.
(bright, bright,)

D

2.

Bridge:

F C

Look all a - round, there's noth - ing but blue skies.

F

Look straight a - head, there's noth - ing but

A C♯m/G♯ G

blue skies.

C♯/G♯
G
C
Bm
A
D.S. 𝄋 al Coda
𝄌 Coda
C
It's gon-na be a bright,
bright,
(bright,
G
D
Repeat ad lib. and fade
bright,)
sun-shin-y day.
It's gon-na be a bright,

JUST WHAT I NEEDED

Words and Music by
RIC OCASEK

C♯m
4fr.
G♯
4fr.
E
I kind of lose my mind.
as long as it was deep.
It's not the per - fume
You al - ways knew to
B
C♯m
4fr.
G♯
4fr.
that you wear;
wear it well
and
it's not the rib - bons in your hair.
you look so fan - cy. I can tell.
E
B
G♯
4fr.
A
I don't mind you com - ing here
I don't mind you hang - ing out
and wast - ing all my time.
and talk - ing in your sleep.
E
B
A
C♯m
4fr.
B
E
B
A
I guess you're just what I need - ed.
I need - ed

C♯m
4fr.
E
B
A
C♯m
B
some - one to feed.
I guess you're just what I need - ed.
E
B
A
C♯m
I need - ed some - one to bleed.
E
B
C♯m
G♯
E
B
C♯m
A
E
B
C♯m
G♯
A
B
C♯m

LAYLA

Words and Music by
ERIC CLAPTON and JIM GORDON

Verse:
C♯m
G♯m
1. (A) what - 'll you do when you get lone - ly,
2. I tried to give you con - so - la - tion
3. So, make the best of the sit - u - a - tion,
C♯m
C7
D7
E7
and no - bod - y's wait - in' by your side?
when your old man, he let you down.
be - fore I fi - n'lly go in - sane.
F♯m
B
E
A
You've been run - nin' and hid - ing much too long.
Like a fool, I fell in love with you.
Please don't say we'll nev - er find a way
F♯m
B
E
N.C.
You know it's just your fool - ish pride.
You turned my whole world up - side down.
or tell me all my love's in vain.
Lay -

Chorus:
Dm
B♭
C
Dm
la,
you got me on my knees.
Lay -
B♭
C
Dm
la,
I beg you, dar - ling, please.
Lay -
B♭
C
Dm
la,
dar - lin', won't you ease my wor-ried
B♭
C
1.2.
mind?

3.
Dm
B♭
C
Lay - la,
you
got me on my knees.
Lay - la,
I
beg you, dar - ling, please.
Lay - la,
dar - lin', won't you ease my wor - ried mind?

B♭
C
Dm
C
(Guitar)
Repeat as desired for solos
Dm
Last time
Interlude:
C
C/E
F
mp
C
C/E
F
mf

B♭9(♭5)
C
C/E
F
B♭9(♭5)
C
Am
Dm
G
C
Am
D
G

C
C/E
F
1.
3
2.
C
C/E
F
3
B♭9(♭5)
C
C
C/E
F
Repeat as desired for solos
3
B♭9(♭5)
C
rit. e dim.
mp

LET IT BLEED

Words and Music by
MICK JAGGER and KEITH RICHARDS

D
F

Yeah, we all___ need some - one we can lean on.___
Yeah, we all___ need some - one we can cream on.___

D7 E7 A *To Coda* ⊕
F7 G7 C

And if you want it, well, you can lean on me.________
And if you want to, well, you can cream on me.________

Verse 1:

C♯7 D
E7 F

1. She said, "My breasts, they will al - ways_ be o - pen.

E7 A
G7 C

Ba - by, you can rest_ your wear - y head right on me.__

C#7
E7
And there will al - ways be a space in my park -
D
F
E7
G7
ing lot when you need a lit - tle
D.S. 𝄋 al Coda
coke and sym - pa - thy."
2. Yeah, we all
Coda
Verse 2:
A
C#7
C
E7
2. I was dream - ing of a steel gui - tar en - gage -

D7 E7
F7 G7

ment_ when you drunk my health_ in scen - ted jas - mine tea.

A C#7
C E7

But__ you knifed__ me in___ my dirt - y, filth - y base-

D7 E7
F7 G7

ment_ with that jad - ed, fad - ed, junk - y nurse. Oh,__ what plea-

Chorus 3:

A7
C7

sant com-pan-y,_____ hah! 3. Don't___ we all____ need some - one we can feed_

D
D7
E7
F
F7
G7
on.
Yeah, and if you want it,
well, you can feed on me.
A7
C7
Hey!
Take my arm,
take my leg,
oh, ba - by, don't you take my head.
A
C
Chorus 4:
Whoo!
4. Yeah, we all need some - one we can

D
D7
E7
F
F7
G7
bleed on.
Yeah, and if you want it, ba - by, well, you can bleed on me.
A
A7
C
C7
Yeah!
We all need some - one we can bleed
D
E7
F
G7
on.
Yeah, yeah, and if you want it, ba - by, why don't - cha bleed on me
A7
C7
all o - ver. Whoo!
(Inst. solo ad lib....

D7
E7
F7
G7
A
C
1.
2.
A7
C7
Ahh,
get it on, rid - er,
...end solo)
whoo!
Get it on, rid - er,
get it on, rid - er,
Repeat ad lib. and fade
you can bleed all o - ver me,
yeah!

LIGHTS

Words and Music by
NEAL SCHON and STEVE PERRY

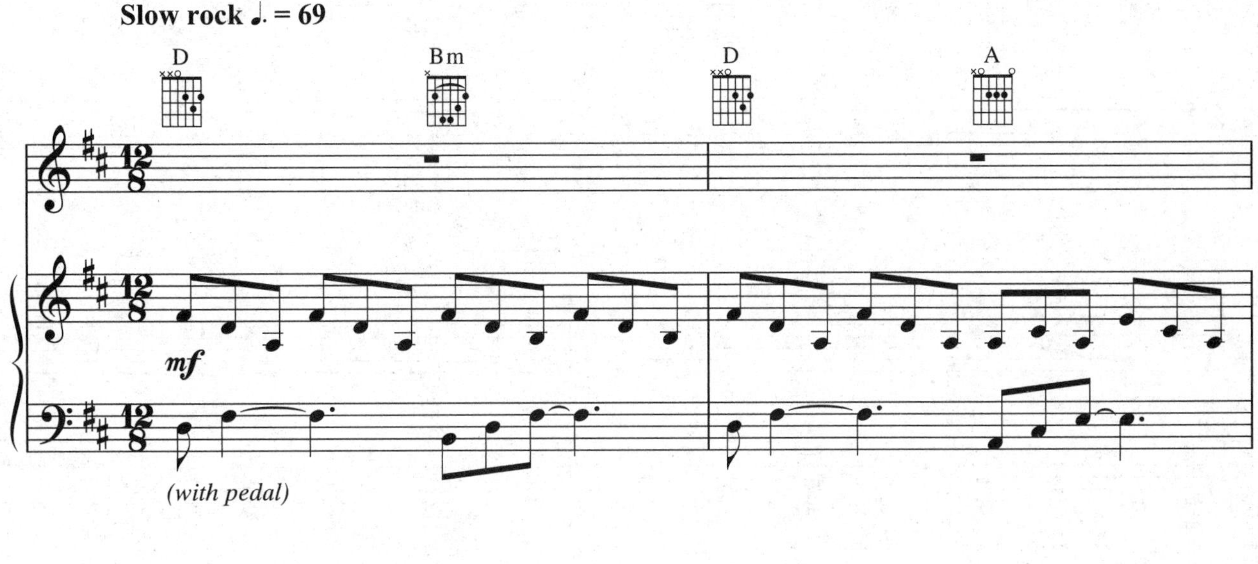

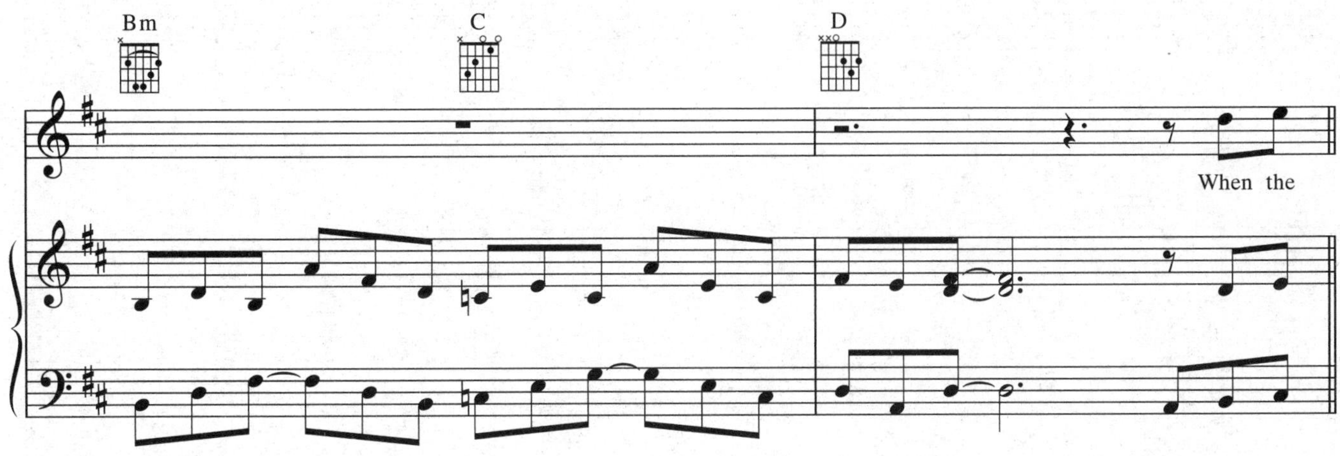

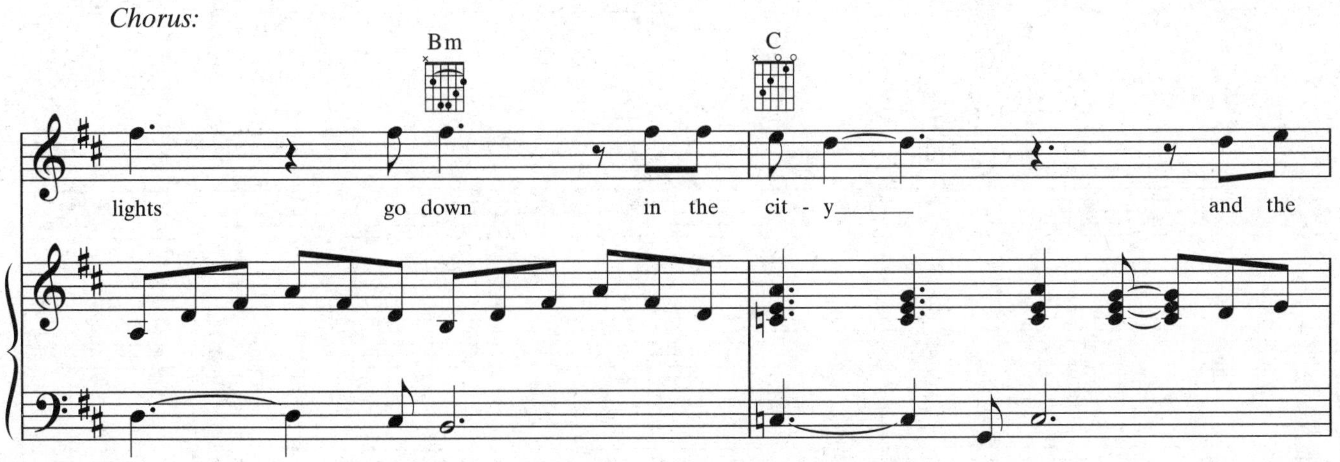

D
Bm
C
D/C
sun shines on the bay,
ooh, I
D
Bm
C
want to be there
in my city,
oh.
Bm
C
D
Oh,
oh,
oh.
Verse:
Bm
C
1. So you think you're lone - ly?

D
Bm
C
Well, my friend, I'm lone - ly too.
D
Bm7
C
I want to get back to my cit - y by the bay - ee - ay.
Bm7
C
D
Oh, oh, oh. It's
Bridge:
Bm
A
G
D
sad, oh, there's been morn - ings out on the road with -
(2nd time - Guitar solo ad lib....
f

Bm
A
G
D
A
F♯/A♯
out you, with - out your charms,
Bm
A
G
D
oh, oh, my, my, my, my, my, my.
Bm7
C
D
Oh, oh, oh.
...end solo)
When the
Chorus:
Bm7
C
lights go down in the cit - y
and the
mf–f

D
Bm7
C
sun shines on the bay,
ooh, I
D
Bm7
C
want to be there in my city,
oh.
Bm7
C
1.
D
Oh, ooh, oh,
oh.
Glissando
2.
D
Bm7
C
D
oh.
Oh, ooh, oh,
oh.
Mmm.

LOLA

Words and Music by
RAY DAVIES

Moderately slow ♩ = 72

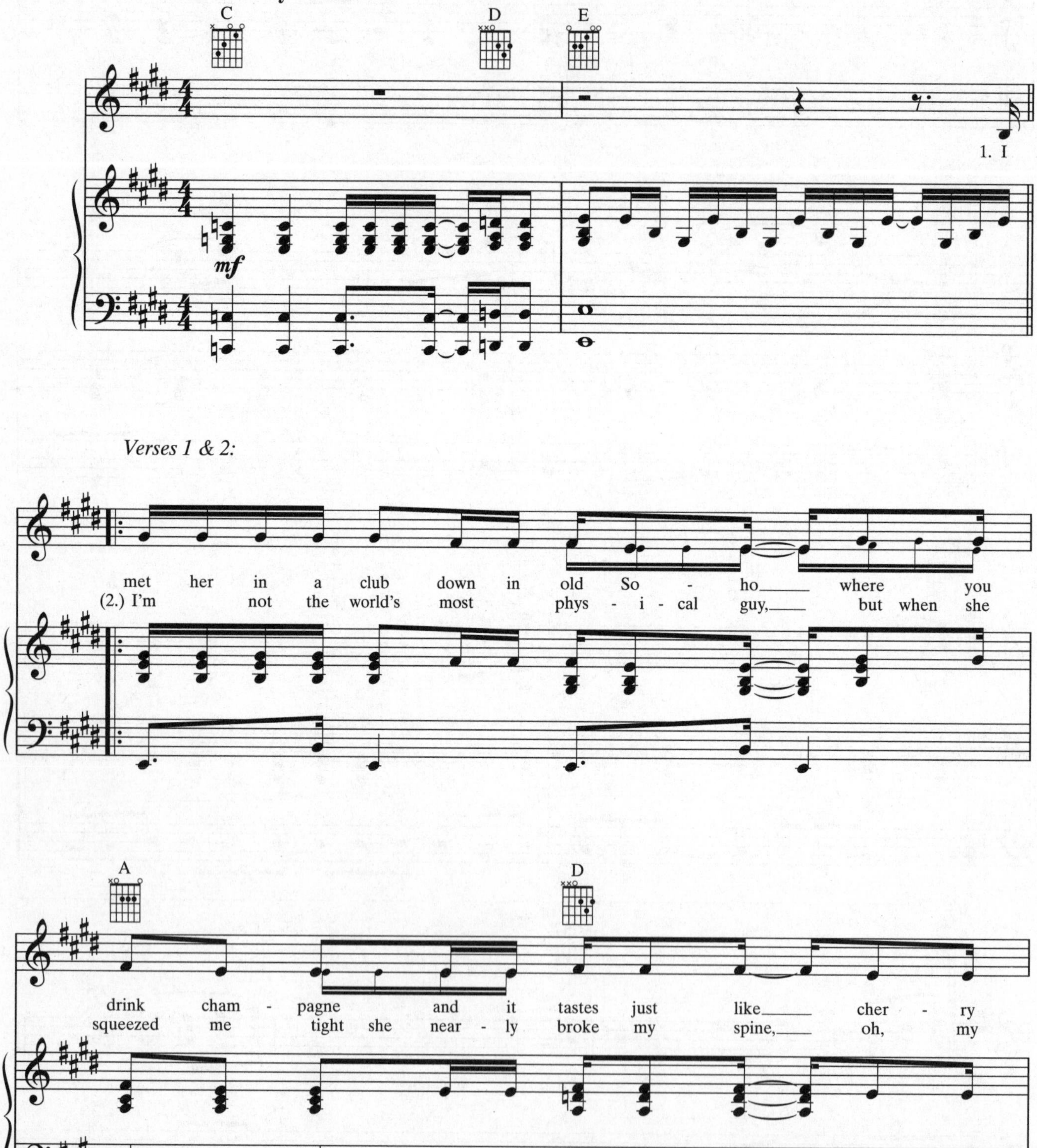

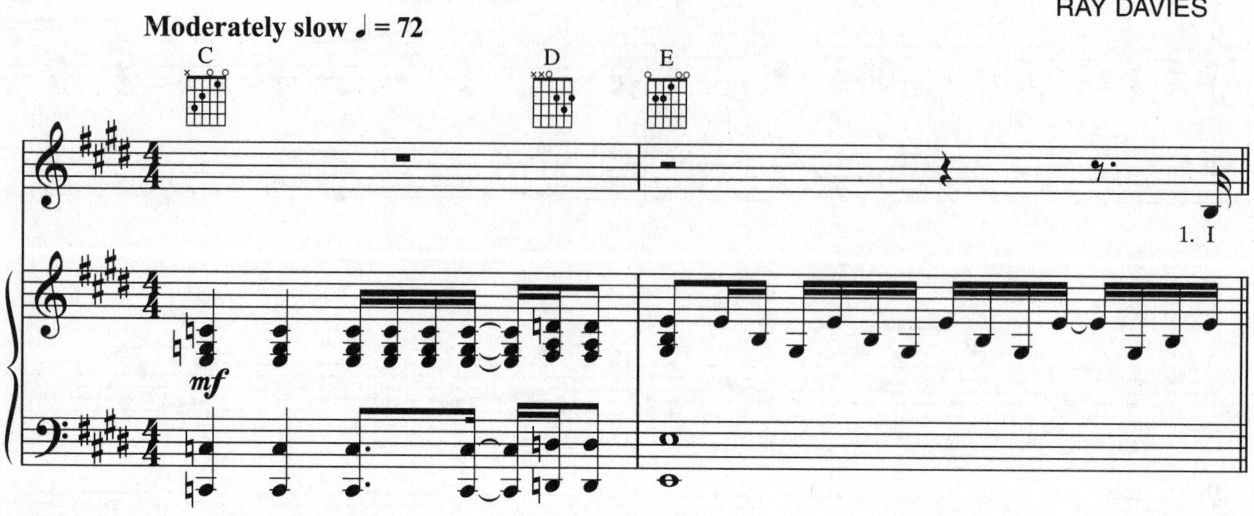

Verses 1 & 2:

met her in a club down in old So - ho where you
(2.) I'm not the world's most phys - i - cal guy, but when she

A D

drink cham - pagne and it tastes just like cher - ry
squeezed me tight she near - ly broke my spine, oh, my

E
A
co - la, c-o - l-a, co - la. She
Lo - la, Lo-lo - lo-lo Lo - la. Well,
E
A
D
walked up to me and she asked me to dance. I asked her her name and in a dark brown voice she said,
I'm not dumb, but I can't un-der-stand why she walked like a wom-an and talked like a man, oh, my
E
A
D
"Lo - la, L-o - l - a, Lo - la, Lo-lo - lo-lo
Lo - la, Lo-lo - lo - lo Lo - la, Lo-lo - lo-lo
C
D
E
Lo - la."
Lo - la."

1.
2.
2. Well,
Well, we
Bridges 1 & 3:
B7
F#7
drank champagne and danced all night under electric candlelight. She
I left home just a week before, and I'd never ever kissed a woman before, when
A
picked me up and sat me on her knee and said, "Dear boy, won't you come home with me?" 3. Well,
Lola smiled and took me by the hand, and said, "Dear boy, I'm gonna make you a man." 5. Well,
Verses 3 & 5:
E
A
D
I'm not the world's most passionate guy, but when I looked in her eyes, well, I almost fell for my
I'm not the world most masculine man, but I know what I am and I'm glad I'm a man and so's

E
A
D
Lo - la, Lo-lo - lo - lo Lo - la, Lo-lo - lo - lo
Lo - la, Lo-lo - lo - lo Lo - la, Lo-lo - lo - lo
C
D
E
Lo - la.
Lo - la, Lo-lo - lo - lo
Lo - la.
Lo - la, Lo-lo - lo - lo
To Coda
A
D
C
D
Lo - la, Lo-lo - lo - lo Lo - la.
Lo - la, Lo-lo - lo - lo
E
I

Bridge 2:
A
C♯m7
B
A
C♯m7
B
pushed her a - way, I walked to the door, I
A
C♯m7
B
E
G♯m7
C♯m
fell to the floor, I got down on my knees. Then
Verse 4:
B
E
I looked at her, and she at me. 4. Well, that's the way that I want it to stay, and I
A
D
E
al - ways want it to be that way for my Lo - la, la la la la,

A E

Lo - la. Girls will be boys, and boys will be girls; it's a

A D E

mixed - up, mud - dled - up, shook - up world ex - cept for Lo - la, Lo - lo - lo - lo

D.S. 𝄋 al Coda

𝄌 Coda

C D

Lo - la. Well, Lo - la.

Repeat ad lib. and fade

E A D C D

Lo - la, Lo - lo - lo - lo Lo - la, Lo - lo - lo - lo Lo - la.

MAGGIE MAY

Words and Music by
ROD STEWART and MARTIN QUITTENTON

Moderately fast ♩ = 132
D
Em
G
D
Dsus2 sus4
mf
D
Em
G
D
Em
F♯m
Verse:
A
G
D
1. Wake up, Mag-gie, I think I got some-thin' to say to you.__ It's
2. 3. 4. See additional lyrics
A
G
D
late Sep - tem-ber and I real - ly should__ be back__ at__ school. I

G
D
G
A
know I keep you a - mused,
but I feel I'm be - ing used.
Oh,
Em
F♯m
Em7
Asus/E
Mag-gie, I could-n't have tried
an - y more.
You
Em
A
Em
led me a - way from home,
just to save you from be-in' a -
A
Em
A
lone.
You stole my heart
and that's
what real - ly hurts.

D
1.2.
3.4.
2. The
Em7
A
D
G
Em7
1.
G
A
D
D.S. 𝄋
2.
G
A
D
3.
G
A
D
Em
G
D
Dsus2 sus4

1.–3. 4.

D Em G D Dsus2 sus4 D Dsus2 sus4

D Em G D Dsus2 sus4

1. Mag- gie, I wish I'd nev - er seen_ your_ face.
(2.) get on back home_____ one of these days.___
3. 4. *(etc.) Instr. repeat ad lib. and fade*

Repeat ad lib. and fade

D Em G D Dsus2 sus4

2. I'll

Verse 2:
The morning sun, when it's in your face, really shows your age.
But that don't worry me none; in my eyes you're ev'rything.
I laughed at all of your jokes; my love you didn't need to coax.
Oh, Maggie, I couldn't have tried any more.
You led me away home, just to save you from being alone.
You stole my soul, and that's a pain I can do without.

Verse 3:
All I needed was a friend to lend a guiding hand.
But you turned into a lover, and, Mother, what a lover! You wore me out.
All you did was wreck my bed, and in the morning kick me in the head.
Oh, Maggie, I couldn't have tried any more.
You led me away home, 'cause you didn't want to be alone.
You stole my heart; I couldn't leave you if I tried.

Verse 4:
I suppose I could collect my books and get on back to school,
Or steal my Daddy's cue and make a living out of playin' pool,
Or find myself a rock 'n' roll band that needs a helpin' hand.
Oh, Maggie, I wish I'd never seen your face.
You made a first-class fool out of me, but I'm as blind as a fool can be.
You stole my heart, but I love you anyway.

MAMA TOLD ME NOT TO COME

Words and Music by
RANDY NEWMAN

Moderate rock (♩ = 112)

* Original recording in A♭ Major

What's all these cra - zy ques - tions they're ask - in' me?
This is the cra - zi - est par - ty that could ev - er be.
Don't turn on the lights 'cause I don't wan - na see.
Ma - ma told
Chorus:
G
G7/B
C
E♭7/D♭
G
G7/B
C
me not to come.
Ma - ma told me not to come.

E♭7/D♭
G
1.
G7/B
C
That ain't the way to have fun, no. Uh - uh.
(3rd time - She said,)
N.C.
2. 3.
mf
That ain't the way to have fun,
son.
To Coda
N.C.
That ain't the way to have fun, son.
(Guitar solo ad lib....

G7/B
C
E♭7/D♭
G
G7
D.S. 𝄋 al Coda
(after 3rd ending)
…end solo)
3. The
Coda
N.C.
That ain't the way to have fun, no.
Shout Chorus:
G
G7/B
C
E♭7/D♭
G
Ma - ma told me, Ma - ma told me, Ma - ma told me, told me, told me.
(3 voices ad lib. freely)
G7/B
C
E♭7/D♭
G
G7/B
C
It's dan - ger - ous, oh yeah, yeah. Ma - ma told me not to go,

E♭7/D♭
G
G7/B
C
oh Ma - ma, Ma - ma. Ma - ma told me.
That ain't the way to have fun, no. That ain't the way to have fun,
son.
(more vocal ad libs.)
That ain't the way to have fun, no. That ain't the way to have fun,

E♭7/D♭ G G7/B C E♭7/D♭ G

son.

N.C.

mf

rit.

Verse 2:
(Spoken:)
Open up the window, let some air into this room.
I think I'm almost chokin' from the smell of stale perfume.
And that cigarette you're smokin' 'bout scare me half to death.
Open up the window, sucker, let me catch my breath.
(To Chorus:)

Verse 3:
(Spoken:)
The radio is blastin', someone's knockin' at the door.
I'm lookin' at my girlfriend; she's passed out on the floor.
I seen so many things I ain't never seen before.
Don't know what it is; I don't wanna see no more.
(To Chorus:)

MARGARITAVILLE

Words and Music by
JIMMY BUFFETT

A
Strum-min' my six - string
But it's a real beau - ty,
But there's booze in the blend - er,
on my front porch swing.
a Mex - i - can cu - tie,
and soon it will ren - der
Smell those shrimp;
how it got
that fro - zen con -
D
they're be - gin - ning to boil.
here I have - n't a clue.
coc - tion that helps me hang on.
Chorus:
G
A
D
D7
Wast-in' a - way a - gain in Mar-ga - ri - ta-ville,

G
A
D
search - in' for my lost shak - er of salt.
D7
G
A
Some people claim that there's a
D
A/C#
G
A
wom - an to blame,
but I know
now I think,
but I know
1.2.
D
it's no - bod - y's fault.
hell, it could be my fault.
it's my own damn fault.

3.
D
G
Yes, and some_ peo - ple claim_
A
D
A/C♯
G
___ that there's_ a wom - an to blame,___ and I know_
A
D
it's my own_ damn_ fault._
G
A
D

MUSTANG SALLY

Words and Music by
BONNY RICE

Moderate R&B ♩ = 116

𝄋 *Verse:*

F7

Sal-ly, no, ba - by, guess you bet-ter slow___ your Mus-tang down._

C7

___ You been

G7 F7

run-nin' all o-ver town,___ now,_ oh, I guess I have to put your flat feet on the

C7

ground._

Chorus:

All you wan - na do is ride a - round, Sal - ly. (Ride, Sal - ly, ride.)
All you wan - na do is ride a - round, Sal - ly.
(Ride, Sal - ly, ride.)
F7
All you wan - na do is ride
a - round, Sal - ly. (Ride, Sal - ly, ride.)
C7
All you wan - na do is a - ride

Verse 2:
I bought you a brand-new Mustang,
'Bout Nineteen sixty-five.
Now you come around, signifying a woman,
You don't wanna let me ride.
Mustang Sally, now, baby,
Guess you better slow that Mustang down.
You been runnin' all over town,
Oh, I've got to put your flat feet on the ground.
(To Chorus:)

PIECE OF MY HEART

Words and Music by
JERRY RAGOVOY and BERT RUSSELL

B
A
E
A
Yeah, and did - n't I give you near - ly ev - 'ry - thing that a wom - an
B
C♯m
pos - si - bly can? Hon - ey, you know I did. But each time I tell my - self that I,
mf
B
D
well, I think I've had e - nough, oh, but I'm gon - na show you, ba - by, that a
B
wom - an can be tough. I want you to come on, come on, come on, come on and

Chorus:
E
A
B
A
take it! Take an - oth - er lit - tle piece of my heart now, ba - by. (Whoa,
f
E
A
B
A
break it!) Break an - oth - er lit - tle bit of my heart. (Whoa,
E
A
B
B♭
have a) Have an - oth - er lit - tle piece of my heart now, ba - by.
A
1.
G♯m
F♯m
E
Well, you know you got it, if it makes you feel good, oh, yes, in - deed.
mp

A
B
A
2.
G♯m
F♯m
E
2. You're makes you feel good.
F♯m
A
B
F♯m
Guitar solo ad lib.
1.
A
B
2.
A
B
C♯m
B
D
B
I want you to

come on, come on, come on, come on and
Chorus:
E
A
B
A
take it! Take an - oth - er lit - tle piece of my heart now, ba - by. (Whoa,
E
A
B
A
break it!) Break an - oth - er lit - tle bit of my heart. (Whoa,
E
A
B
B♭
have a) Have an - oth - er lit - tle piece of my heart now, ba - by.

Verse 2:
You're out on the streets lookin' good,
And, baby, deep down in your heart
I guess you know that it ain't right.
Never, never, never, never, never,
Never hear me when I cry at night,
Baby, I cry all the time.
But each time I tell myself that I,
Well, I can't stand the pain.
But when you hold me in your arms,
I'll sing it once again.
I said come on, come on, come on, come on and…
(To Chorus:)

RIGHT NOW

Words and Music by
SAMMY HAGAR, ALEX VAN HALEN,
MICHAEL ANTHONY and EDWARD VAN HALEN

B♭
C2
Dm
Dsus
Dm
D2
C
Csus
C
B♭
Dm
C
F
G
B♭
C
Dm
Dsus
Dm
D2
C
Csus
C
B♭
Dm
C
F
G
B♭
C
Dm
Dsus
Dm
D2
C
Csus
C
B♭
Dm

1.
C
F
G
B♭
C
2.
C
B♭
Am
Gm
F
Dm
Verse:
C
B♭
1. Don't wan - na wait_ till to - mor - row.
2. See additional lyrics
A5
G5
A5
G5
A5
C6
Dm
Why put it off an - oth - er day?___
C
B♭
One by one, girl, prob - lems build up_

A5
G5
A5
G5
A5
C6
B♭
and stand in our way.
Oh!
Pre-chorus:
C
F
G
B♭
1. One step a - head, one step be - hind it.
2. See additional lyrics
(3.) now. (Inst. solo ad lib.…
C
Dm
Now, you got - ta run to get e - ven.
B♭
C
F
G
B♭
Make fu - ture plans, don't live a - bout yes - ter - day, hey!

C
Asus
A
Come on, turn, turn this thing a-round. Right
Chorus:
F
F/A
B♭
C7sus
C
now! Hey, it's your to-mor-row. Right
now! Come on, it's ev-'ry-thing. Right
now! Catch your mag-ic mo-ment, do it right here and now.
To Coda

B♭2
1.
2.
It means ev - 'ry - thing.
It means ev - 'ry - thing.
Dm
It's en - light - en - ing.
B♭
Right now.
Dm
Ah, what are you wait - in' for?

B♭
C2
Oh,
F5
G5
B♭
C2
yeah.
A
D.S. 𝄋 al Coda
Right
Coda
F
F/A
B♭
C7sus
C
Oh,
right
now.

Verse 2:
Miss a beat, you lose the rhythm,
And nothing falls into place.
Only missed by a fraction,
Sent a little off your pace.

Pre-chorus 2:
The more things you get, the more you want,
Just tradin' one for the other.
Workin' so hard to make it easy.
Got to turn, come on, turn this thing around.
(To Chorus:)

ROUNDABOUT

Words and Music by
JON ANDERSON and STEVE HOWE

*Guitar adapted for keyboard.

Verse:
Omit harmony vocal 1st time only.
Em F♯m G F♯m G F♯m Em
1. I'll be the round - a - bout;
2. The mu - sic dance and sing,
3. I will re - mem - ber you,
4. I'll be the round - a - bout;
F♯m G F♯m G F♯m Em
the words will make you out and out,
they make the chil - dren real - ly ring.
your sil - hou - ette will charge the view
the words will make you out and out,
F♯m G F♯m G F♯m Am7 Bm7 Cmaj7 Bm7
I'll spend the day your way.
I spend the day your way.
of dis - tant at - mo - sphere.
you spend the day your way.
Cmaj7 Gmaj9 Am7 Bm Bm7/A Gmaj7
Call it morn - ing driv - ing through the sun and in and out the
3. in the sun and e - ven in the
Organ:

1.
Fmaj9/G
Em
F♯m
G
F♯m
G
F♯m Em
val - ley.
F♯m
G
F♯m Bm7
Em
2.3.4.
Fmaj9/G
val - ley.
Synths:
Chorus:
G
C
F
C
F
C G
C
F
C
B♭
In and a - round the lake, moun - tains come out of the sky, and they stand
(Tacet 1st time; play cues 2nd and 3rd times only)

G
C
F
C
F
C
G
there.
One
C
F
C
B♭
G
C
F
C
mile o - ver we'll be there and we'll see you.
(Play every time)
F
C
G
C
F
C
B♭
G
Ten true sum-mers we'll be there and laugh - ing too.

C F C F C G C F C B♭
Twen - ty-four be - fore my love, you'll
see, I'll be there with you.
Am/E Bm/E C/E D/E Em7
To Coda 1.
F#m7 Gmaj7 F#m7 Gmaj7 F#m7 Em7 F#m7 Gmaj7 F#m9 Bm7
Synths:

Em7
F♯m7
Gmaj7
F♯m7
Gmaj7 F♯m7 Em7
D.S. 𝄋
N.C.
Organ:
2.
N.C.
Organ:

N.C.
Play 3 times
A - long the drift - ing cloud,_ the ea - gle search - ing down_ on the land.
Catch - ing the swirl - ing wind,_ the sail - or sees the rim___ of the land.
The ea - gle's danc - ing wings_ cre - ate as weath - er spins_ out of hand.
Play 3 times
Go clos - er hold the land,_ feel part - ly no more than_grains of sand.
We stand to lose all time,_ a thou - sand an - swers by___ in our hand.
Next to your deep - er fears,_ we stand sur - round - ed by a mil - lion years.

I'll be the round - a - bout;
the words will make
you out and out.
you out and out.
1.
2.
ppp
rit.
Freely, slowly
Em
p
mp

C
Em

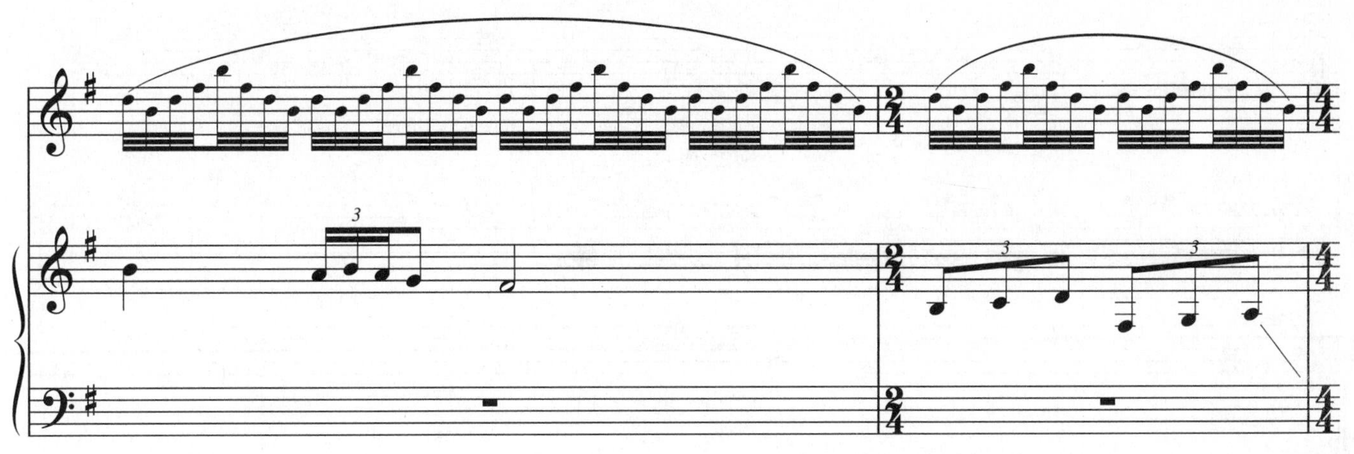

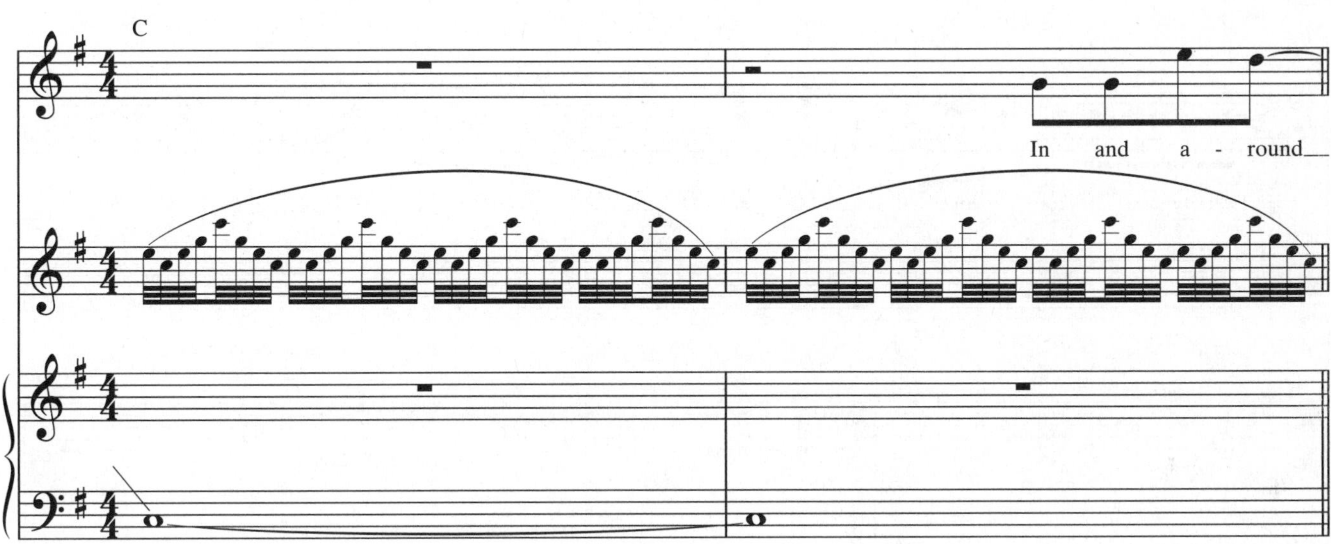
C
In and a - round

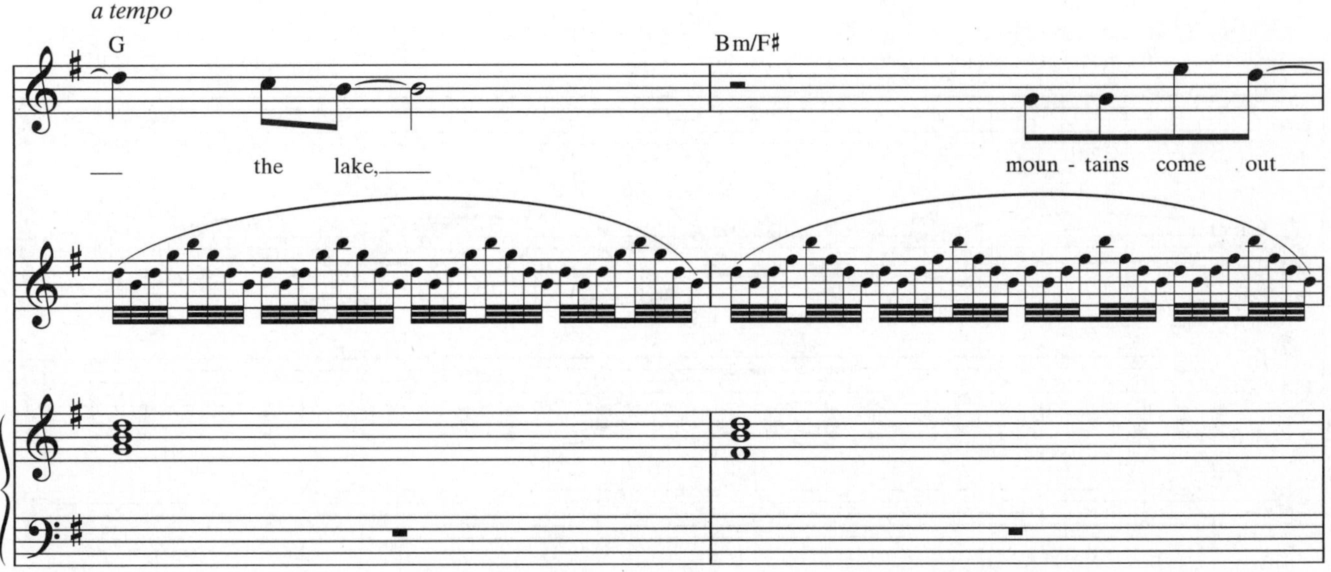
a tempo
G
Bm/F♯
the lake,
moun - tains come out

Em
B♭
of the sky,
they
stand there.
G
F
B♭
E♭
Twen-ty-four be-fore my love and
I'll
be
there.
G C F C F C G C F C B♭
Organ solo:
mf

G C F C F C G
C F C B♭ G C F C
F C G C F C B♭
G C F C F C G C F C B♭

G
B♭/F
G
B♭/F
3
G
B♭/F
Guitar solo:
G
B♭/F

G C F C F C G C F C B♭
Organ solo:
G C F C F C G
C F C B♭ G
F G

F
G
F
Guitar solo:
G
F
N.C.
D.S.𝄋 al Coda
F♯sus
Em
Coda
Em
Da da da da da
da
da.
Da da da da da
mp

Da da da. Da da da. Da
da da. da. Da da da da da da da. Da da da da da
da da. Da da da. Da da da. Da da da.
da da. Da da da da da da da. Da da da da da
Da da da. Da da da. Da da da. Da
da da. Da da da da da da da. Da da da da da
D C Bm Am G F♯m E
da da. Da.
da da.

RUNNING ON EMPTY

Words and Music by
JACKSON BROWNE

D/A
A
Look - ing out at the road rush - ing un - der my wheels.
Got - ta do what you can just to keep your
Look - ing out at the road rush - ing un - der my wheels.
D/A
A
D/A
love a - live,
Look - ing back at the years
try - in' not to con - fuse
I don't know how to tell
A
D/A
A
gone by like so man - y sum - mer fields.
it with what you do to sur - vive.
you all just how cra - zy this life feels.

D/A
A
In six - ty - five I was sev - en - teen and
In six - ty - nine I was twen - ty - one and I
I look a - round for the friends that I used to
D/A
A
D
run - ning up one - o - one.
called the road my own.
turn to to pull me through.
I don't know where I'm
I don't know when that road
Look - ing in - to their eyes,
A/C♯
2 fr.
E
run - ning now; I'm just run - ning on.
turned on - to the road I'm on.
I see them run - ning too.
Run - ning on,

D/A
A
D/A
A
Run-ning on emp - ty.
Run-ning blind.
run-ning on,
D/A
A
Run - ning in - to the sun,
run - ning on,
F#m
but I'm run-ning be - hind.
To Coda
but I'm run-ning be - hind.

D/A
A
D/A
A
D/A
A
F#m
D
A/C#
2 fr.
E
F#m
D
E
A
Ev-'ry-one I know,
ev-'ry-where I go,

F♯m
E
D
peo-ple need some rea - son to be - lieve. I don't know a-bout
A
F♯m
D
E
an-y-one but me. If it takes all night,
A
D
that-'ll be all right, if I can get you to smile
E
D
A/C♯
2 fr.
Bm7
A
D.S. 𝄋
(no repeats)
al Coda 𝄌
be-fore I leave.

Coda
D/A
A
Hon - ey, you real - ly tempt ___ me, ___ you know, the
way you look _ so kind. ___
I'd love to stick a - round, _
E
D
A/C#
2 fr.
Bm7
_ but I'm run - ning be - hind. ___
Run - ning on. _
You know, I don't e - ven know ___ what I'm hop - in' to find.

D
A/C♯
2 fr.
Bm7
A
Run-ning blind.
Run-ning in-to the sun,
E
but I'm run-ning be-hind.
D/A

SHE'S A RAINBOW

Words and Music by
MICK JAGGER and KEITH RICHARDS

Chorus:
E♭
B♭sus B♭
B♭sus B♭
she combs her hair. She's like a rain - bow,
B♭sus B♭
E♭
B♭
com-ing, col-ors in the air. Oh, ev'ry - where, she comes in
F7
B♭
To Coda
col - ors. Wanh, wanh, la-la - la.
freely

Bassoon
F7
tr
a tempo
tr
tr
tr
B♭ Guitar
to Strings
E♭ Strings
B♭

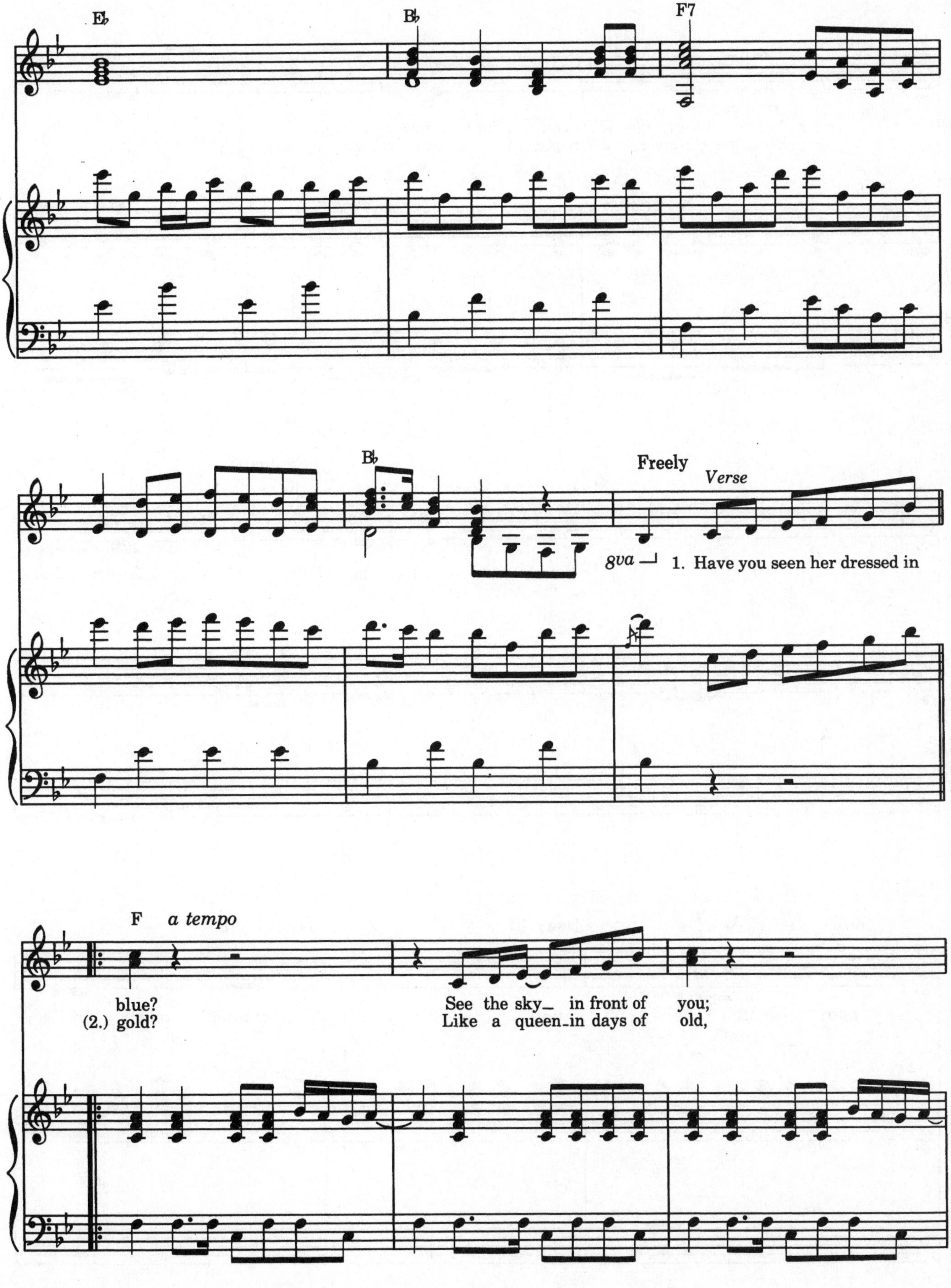

E♭
B♭
F7
B♭
Freely
Verse
8va
1. Have you seen her dressed in
F
a tempo
blue?
(2.) gold?
See the sky_ in front of you;
Like a queen_in days of old,

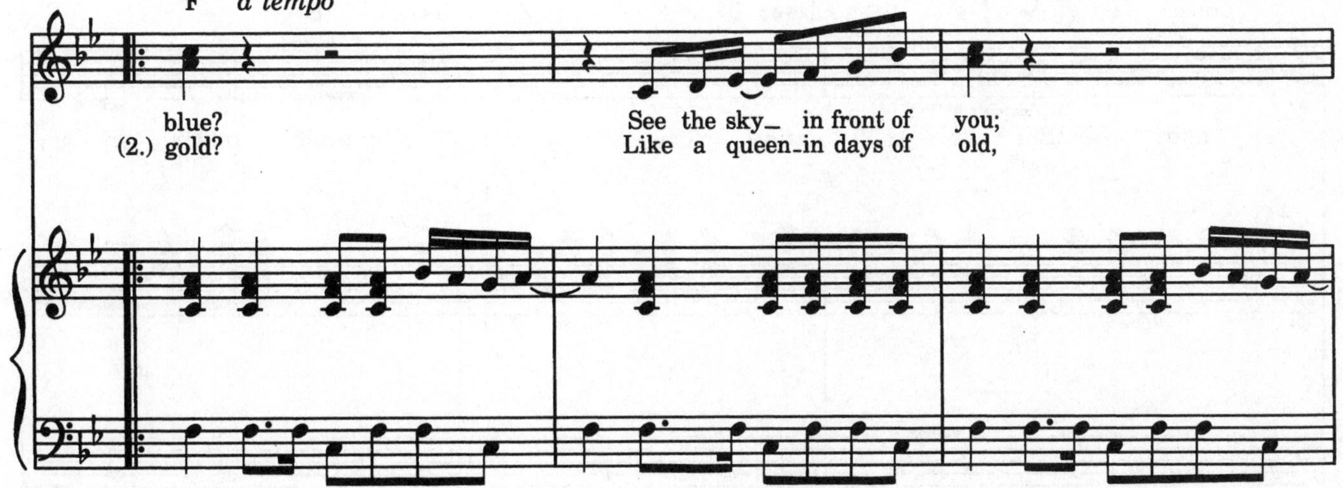

F
and her face is like a sail, speck of white so fair and pale.
She shoots her col-ors all a - round like a sun - set go - ing down.
Have you seen a la - dy
B♭sus B♭
fair - er?
B♭sus B♭
She comes in col-ors ev-'ry - where;
Chorus
E♭sus E♭
she combs her
B♭sus B♭
hair. She's like a rain - bow,
B♭sus B♭
B♭sus B♭
com-ing, col-ors in the

E♭
B♭sus
B♭
F7
air. Oh, ev - 'ry - where, she comes in col ors
B♭
1.
2. D. S. 𝄋 al Coda
Bassoon
Ooh, wah wah la la.
2. Have you seen her all in
Strings
Coda
B♭
Guitar

SHOWER THE PEOPLE

Words and Music by
JAMES TAYLOR

G
D
A
Bb
F
C
One thing can lead to an - oth - er; it does-n't
Once you tell some-bod-y the way that you feel you can
Bm
D/A
G
D
Dm
F/C
Bb
F
take an - y sac - ri - fice. Oh, fa - ther and moth - er, sis -
feel it be-gin-ning to ease. I think it's true what they say a-bout the
A
A#07
Bm
D/A
G
D/F#
C
C#07
Dm
F/C
Bb
F/A
ter and broth - er, if it feels nice don't think twice. Just
squeak - y wheel, al-ways get - ting the grease. Bet - ter to
Em7
A
Em7
Gm7
C
Gm7
show-er the peo - ple you love with love;
show them the way that you feel.

A
Em7
A
A#o7
C
Gm7
C
C#o7
Things are gon - na {work out / be just} fine, if you on - ly will.
Bm
F#o7
Em7
A
Dm
Ao7
Gm7
C
Show-er the peo-ple you love with love;
Em7
A
Em7
Gm7
C
Gm7
show them the way you feel.
Things are gon-na be much bet-
A
A#o7
1.
Bm
C
G
C
C#o7
Dm
Eb
Bb
ter if you on - ly will.

Vocal Ad Lib

They say in every life,
They say the rain must fall.
Just like a pouring rain,
Make it rain.
Love is sunshine.

STAIRWAY TO HEAVEN

Words and Music by
JIMMY PAGE and ROBERT PLANT

C
D
Fmaj7
Am
C
D
Fmaj7
1. There's a
Verse 1:
Am
E+/G♯
C/G
D/F♯
Fmaj7
la - dy who's sure all that glit - ters is gold, and she's buy - ing a stair-way to
G/B Am
Am
E+/G♯
C/G
D/F♯
heav - en. When she gets there, she knows if the stores are all closed, with a
Fmaj7
G/B Am
C
D
word she can get what she came for. Ooo,

Fmaj7
Am
C
G
Dsus
D
ooo, ooo, and she's buy - ing a stair - way to heav - en. There's a
C
D
Fmaj7
Am
C
D
sign on the wall, but she wants to be sure, 'cause you know some - times words have two
Fmaj7
Am
E+/G♯
C/G
D/F♯
mean - ings. In a tree by the brook, there's a song - bird who sings, some - times
Fmaj7
G/B
Am
Am
E+/G♯
all of our thoughts are mis - giv - en.

C/G
D/F♯
Fmaj7
G/B
Am
G/B
Slightly faster
Am7
Dsus
D
Am7
Em/D
Ooo, it makes me won - der.
D
C/D
D
Am7
Dsus
D
Ooo, makes me won - der.
Am7
Em/D
D
C/D
D
2. There's a

Verses 2 & 3:
C
G/B
Am
C
G/B
Fmaj7
feel - ing I get when I look to the west, and my spir - it is cry - ing for leav -
whis - pered that soon if we all call the tune, then the pip - er will lead us to rea -
Am
C
G/B
Am
3
ing. In my thoughts I have seen rings of smoke through the trees, and the
son. And a new day will dawn, for those who stand long, and the
C
G/B
Fmaj7
Am
C
G/B
voic - es of those who stand look - ing.
for - ests will ech - o with laugh - ter.
Am7
Dsus
D
Am7
Em/D
Ooh, it makes me won - der.

D C/D D Am7 Dsus D

Ooo, ___ it real-ly makes me won - der.

Am7 Em/D 1. D C/D D 2. D C/D D

3. And it's

accel.

Faster (♩ = 88)

Verses 4 & 5:

C G/B Am C G/B Fmaj7

4. If there's a bus - tle in your hedge-row, don't be a - larmed now, it's just a spring clean for the May ___
5. Your head is hum-ming and it won't go, in case you don't know, the pip-er's call - ing you to join ___

mf

Am C G/B Am

___ Queen. Yes, there are two paths you can go by, but in the long run,
___ him. Dear la - dy, can you hear the wind blow, and did you know,

C
G/B
Fmaj7
Am
C
G/B
there's still time to change the road you're on.
your stair-way lies on the whis - p'rin' wind.
1.
Am7
Dsus
D
Am7
Em/D
And it makes me won - der,
D
C/D
D
Am7
Dsus
D
ahh.
Am7
Em/D
D
C/D
D
2.
D

D2
D
Dsus
D2
D
Dsus
D
C(9)
C(9)#11
C(9)
C(9)#11
C(9)
f
D2
D
Dsus
D2
D
Dsus
D
C(9)
C(9)#11
C(9)
G/B
Guitar Solo:
Am
C/G
F
Fmaj7
Am
C/G
F
Fmaj7
Am
C/G
F
Fmaj7

Am
C/G
F
Fmaj7
Am
C/G
F
Fmaj7
Am
C/G
F
Fmaj7
Am
C/G
Fmaj7
Am
C/G

Fmaj7
Am
C/G
Fmaj7
Am
C/G
Fmaj7
3
Am
G
F
G
Am
G
And as we wind_ on down the road,__
our shad - ows tall - er than our soul.__
F
G
Am
G
F
G
There walks a la - dy we all know,____

Am
G
F
G
Am
G
who shines white light and wants to show_
how ev - 'ry - thing_ still turns to
F
G
Am
G
F
G
gold.
And if you lis - ten ver - y hard,
Am
G
F
G
Am
G
Fmaj7
the tune will come to you_ at last.
When all are one_ and one is all,_

Am
G
Fmaj7
to be a rock_ and not to roll.
Am
C/G
Fmaj7
Am
C/G
Fmaj7
Am
C/G
Fmaj7
Am
C/G
rit.
Fmaj7
N.C.
And she's buy - ing a stair - way_ to heav - en._
mf

SUNDOWN

Words and Music by
GORDON LIGHTFOOT

* Guitarists: Please note that the chord diagrams are in the key of E but the piano accompaniment is in the key of F. In order for the guitar to sound in the same key as the piano, use a capo on the 1st fret. You also may adjust the capo to play in any key that fits your own individual vocal range.

D
E5
E♭
F
find you bin creep-in' round my back stairs.
find you bin creep-in' round my back stairs.
Sun - down, you
Some - times I
A
D
E5
B♭
E♭
F
bet-ter take care if I find you bin creep-in' round my back stairs.
think it's a sin when I feel like I'm win-nin' when I'm los-in' a-gain.
E5
F
She's bin look-in' like a queen in a sail-or's dream, and she
I can see her look-in' fast in her fad-ed jeans; she's a
B7sus4
E5
C7sus4
F
don't al-ways say what she real-ly means.
hard lov-in' wom-an, got me feel-in' mean.
Some - times I
Some - times I

A
B♭
D
E♭
think it's a shame — when I get feel - in' bet - ter when I'm
think it's a shame — when I get feel - in' bet - ter when I'm
E5
F
A
B♭
feel - in' no pain. — Some - times I think it's a shame. when I
feel - in' no pain. — Sun - down, you bet - ter take care — if I
D
E♭
To Coda
E5
F
get feel - in' bet - ter when I'm feel - in' no pain. —
find you bin creep - in' round
D. S. al Coda
I can

Coda

E5 F — A B♭

my back stairs. Sun - down, you bet-ter take care if I

D E♭ — E5 F

find you bin creep-in' round my back stairs. Some-times I

A B♭ — D E♭ — E5 F

think it's a sin when I feel like I'm win-nin' when I'm los-in' a - gain.

A B♭ — D E♭ — E5 F

SUNSHINE OF YOUR LOVE

Words and Music by
JACK BRUCE, PETE BROWN
and ERIC CLAPTON

Moderately ♩ = 102
N.C.
mf
D
10
C
8
D
10
N.C.
Verse:
1. It's get - ting near dawn,
(2. 4.) with you, my love,
3. (Inst. solo ad lib....
when lights close their tir - ed eyes.
I'll
the light's shin - ing through on you.
Yes, I'm

D
C
D
N.C.
soon be with you, my love, to give you my dawn sur - prise.
with you, my love, it's the morn-ing and just we two.
G
F
G
N.C.
I'll be with you, dar - ling, soon, I'll
I'll stay with you, dar - ling, now, I'll
be with you when the stars start fall - ing.
stay with you till my seas are dried up.
To Coda

Chorus:
A
C
G
A
C
G
I've__ been wait - ing so__ long
to__ be where__ I'm go - ing
A
C
G
A
1.
in__ the sun - shine of__ your love.
D
C
D
N.C.
2.
3.
2. I'm
...end solo)
D
C
D
N.C.
D
C
D
N.C.
D.S. 𝄋 al Coda
4. I'm

Coda
A
C
G
A
C
G
I've been wait - ing so long,
I've been wait - ing so long.
A
C
G
A
C
G
I've been wait - ing so long
to be where I'm go - ing
A
C
G
A
in the sun - shine of your love.
Repeat and fade

SYMPATHY FOR THE DEVIL

Words and Music by
MICK JAGGER and KEITH RICHARDS

A
E
man-y a man's soul and faith.
saw it was a time for a change.
I was a-round when Je-
Killed the Tzar and his
D
A/C♯
A
E
-sus Christ had His mo-ment of doubt and pain.
min-is-ters; An-a-sta-sia screamed in vain.
D
A/C♯
A
Made damn sure that Pi-late washed his hands and sealed His
I rode a tank held a gen-'rals rank when the blitz-krieg raged and the bod-
E
Esus
E
B
fate.
-ies stank.
Pleased to meet you

A
E
A/E
E
hope you guess my name.
Oh yeah.
But
Ah
what's
B
E/B
1.
B
A
E
Esus
puz-zling you is the na - ture of my game.
E
2.
B
A
E
A/E
na-ture of my game. Oh yeah.

E
Esus
E
3. I watched with glee while your
D
A/C♯
A
E
Esus
kings and queens fought for ten de-cades for the Gods they made. I
E
D
A/C♯
A
shout-ed out "Who killed the Ken-ne-dy's?" when af-ter all it was
E
Esus
E
D
you and me. Let me please in-tro-duce my-self I'm a man

A/C♯
A
E
Esus
E
— of wealth — and taste. —
And I lay traps for
D
A/C♯
A
E
Esus
trou-ba - dours —
who get
killed be-fore they reach — Bom - bay. —
E
B
A
Pleased to meet you,
hope you guess my
E
Esus
E
B
E/B
name.
Oh
yeah. —
But what's puz-zling you — is the

* 8va if played by Guitar

D7
G/D
D
A7/C♯
D/A
A
E7
A/E
E
B
E/B
Pleased to meet you
hope you guess my name.
But what's con -
3

B
E/B
B
A
E
A/E
fus-in you is just the na-ture of my game.
E
D
4. Just as ev-ery cop is a crim-i-nal and all
A/C♯
A
E
A
E
the sin- ners, Saints.
As heads is tails, Just call me

D
A/C♯
A
E
A
Lu-ci-fer 'cause I'm in need of some re - straint. So if you
E
D
A/C♯
A
meet me, have some cour - te-sy have some sym-pa-thy and some
E
D
taste. Use all your well learned pol-i - tesse or I'll
A/C♯
A
E
E
E
lay your soul to waste.

B
E/B
A
E
A/E
Pleased to meet_ you ___ hope you guess_my name.
E
B
E/B
B
A
But what's puz-zling you_ is the na-ture of_ my
E
A/E
E
E7
A/E
E
game.
Repeat ad lib. and fade
D7
G/D
D
A7/C♯
D/A
A
E7
A/E
E

TAXI

Words and Music by
HARRY CHAPIN

Moderately ♩ = 116

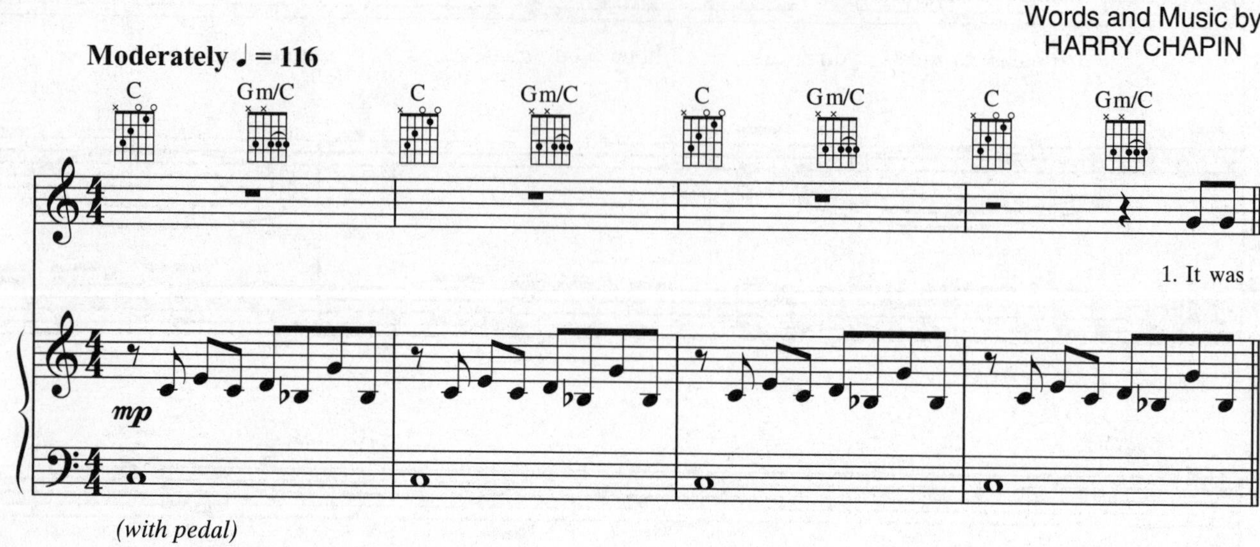
C
Gm/C
mp
(with pedal)
1. It was

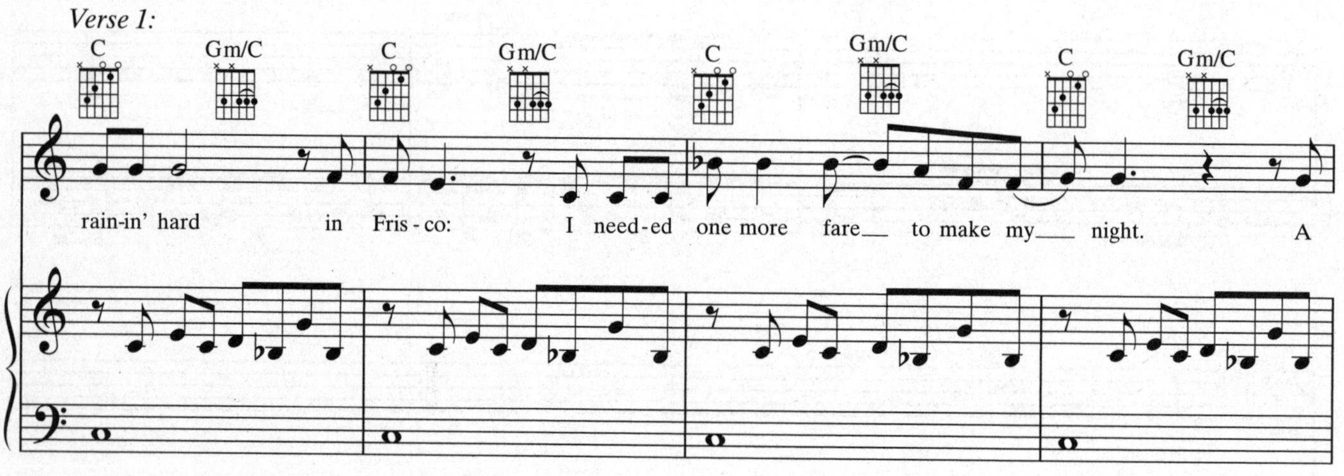
Verse 1:
C
Gm/C
rain-in' hard in Fris-co: I need-ed one more fare to make my night. A

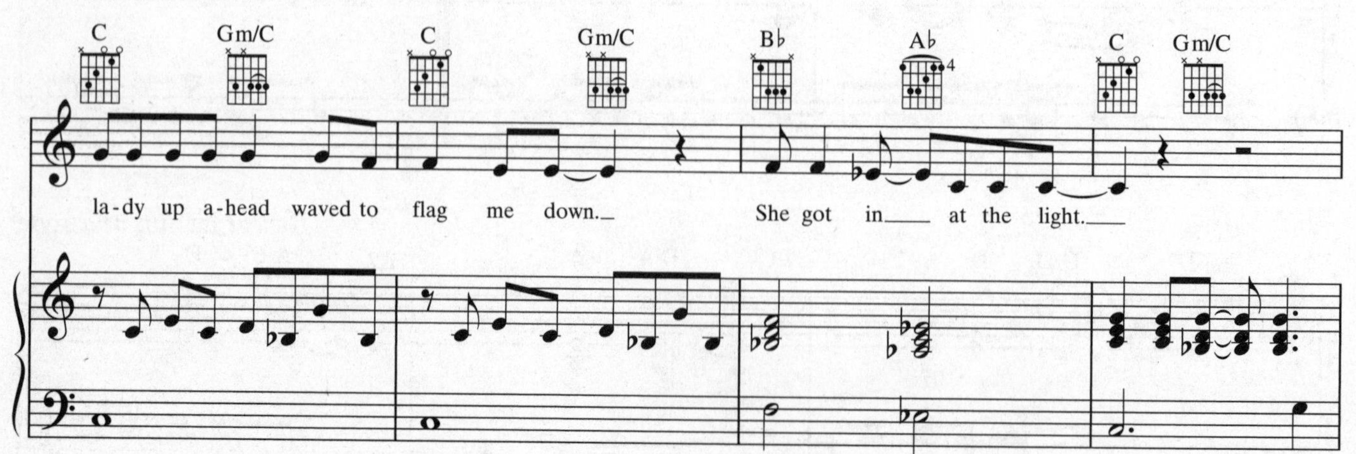
C
Gm/C
B♭
A♭
la-dy up a-head waved to flag me down. She got in at the light.

Verse 2:
C
Gm/C
2. "Oh, where___ you go-ing to, my La-dy Blue? It's a shame you___ ruined your___ gown___ in the rain."
She just looked_ out the win-dow, she said,
B♭
A♭
"Six-teen Park - side Lane."
mf
D
Verses 3 & 6:
Am/D
3. Some-thing a - bout___ her was fa -
6. See additional lyrics

D
Am/D
C
B♭
mil-iar. I could swear I seen her face be-fore.
But she said, "I'm sure you're mis-
tak-en." And she did-n't say an-y-thing more.
4. It took a while,
Verses 4 & 7:
but she looked in the mir - ror. Then she glanced at the li - cense for my name. A
7. See additional lyrics
smile seems to come to her slow-ly. It was a sad smile just the same.
To Coda

Chorus:
D
Am/D
G
D
C
G
And she said, "How_ are you, Har-ry?" I_____ said, "How are you, Sue?_
D
G
D
Bm
Em7
__ Through the too man-y miles__ and the too lit-tle smiles,_ I still_____
Em7/A
D
Am/D
D
Am/D
D
Am/D
__ re-mem-ber you."
3
D
Am/D
D
Am/D
D
Am/D
C
B♭

Verse 5:
D
Am/D
5. It was some-where in a fair-y-tale; I
used to take her home in my car. We learned a-bout love in the back of a Dodge; the
C
B♭
G
Chorus:
les-son had-n't gone too far. You see, she was gon-na be an
Em
Bm
ac - tress, and I was gon-na learn to fly. She took off to find the

D
C
B♭
D
Am/D
D
foot-lights;
I took off to find the sky.
C
cresc.
Bridge:
C
Bm
Whoa, I've got some-thing in-side me to drive a prin-cess
f
E7
Am
Am/G
F♯m7(♭5)
Am/G
Am
F♯m7(♭5)
Am
blind. There's a wild - man wiz - ard; he's hid-ing in me,

D
Em
C
il - lu - mi - nat - ing my mind. Whoa, I've got some-
Bm
E7
Am
Am/G
F♯m7(♭5)
thing in - side me, not what my life's a - bout. 'Cause I've been let - tin'
Am/G
Am
Am/G
F♯m7(♭5)
B♭maj7
my out - side tide me o - ver till my time runs
(O - ver till my time.
decresc.
mf
E♭maj7
out.
)

B♭maj7
F
Cmaj7
(Sung falsetto)
Ba - by's so high that she's sky - ing,
yes, she's
Gm9
C7
fly - ing,
a-fraid to fall.
F
Em7
I'll tell you why ba - by's cry - ing:
'cause she's

Am9
Gm9
dy - ing, are - n't all?
decresc.
D.S. 𝄋 al Coda
Coda
D
Am/D
D
Am/D
D
Am/D
6. There was
8. Well, an -
a tempo
Verse 8:
D5
oth - er man might have been an - gry,
and an - oth - er man might have been hurt.
mf
sim.
But an - oth - er man nev - er would have let her go.

C
B♭
D
Am/D
D
Am/D
I stashed the bill in my shirt.
And she
Chorus:
G
D
C
G
D
walked a-way in si - lence, it's strange how you nev-er know.
But
G
D
Bm
Em7
Em7/A
we'd both got-ten what we asked for such a long, long time a -
Verse 9:
D
Am/D
D
Am/D
D
Am/D
D
Am/D
go.
9. You see, she was gon-na be an ac- tress and

D
Am/D
I was gon-na learn to fly.
She took off to find the foot-lights.
C
B♭
Chorus:
G
I took off for the sky.
And here she's act - ing hap -
Em
Bm
py in - side her hand-some home,
and me, I'm fly-ing in my
tax - i, tak-ing tips and get - ting stoned.
I go

Outro:

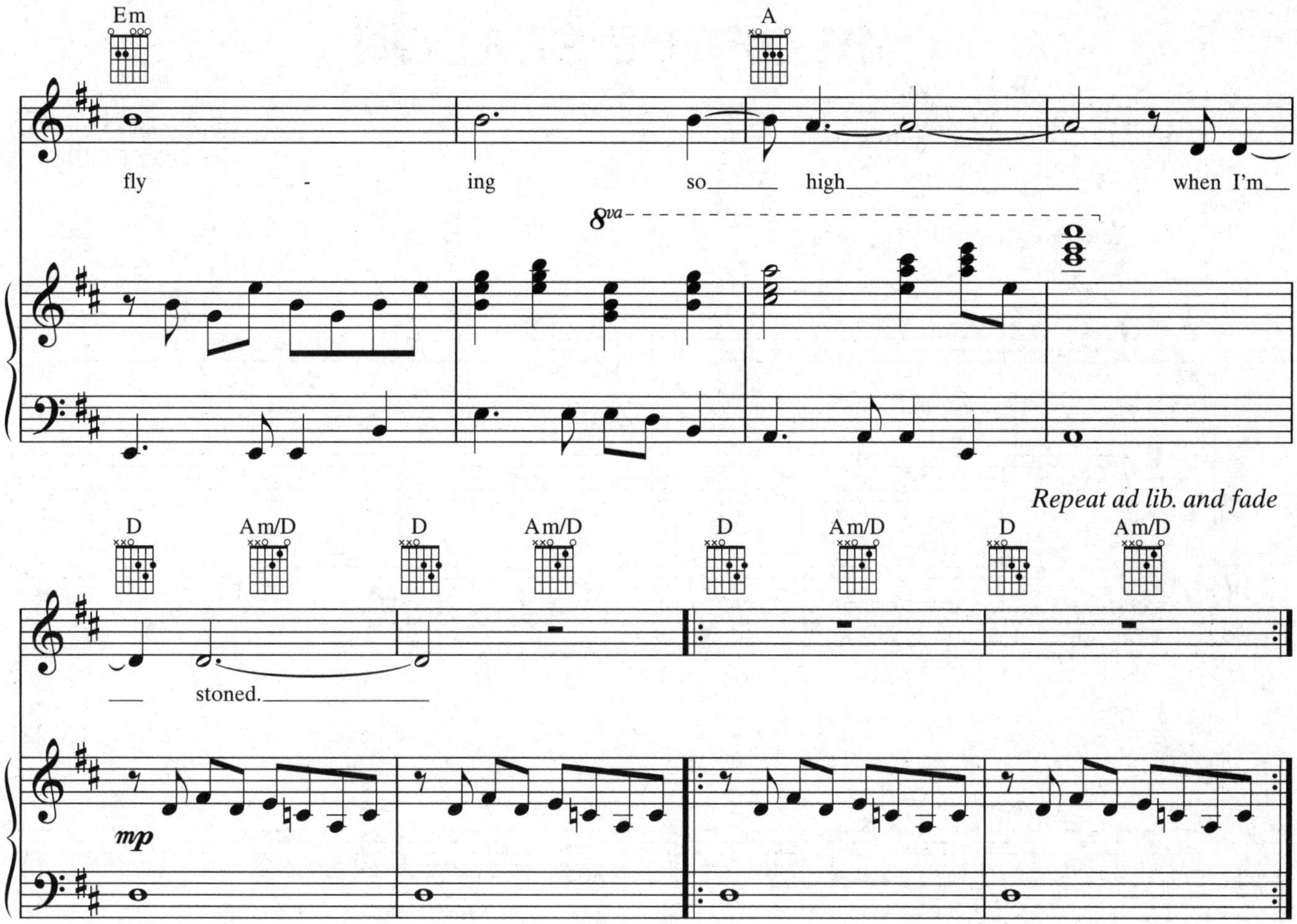

Em A

fly - ing so high when I'm

8va

D Am/D D Am/D D Am/D D Am/D

Repeat ad lib. and fade

stoned.

mp

Verse 6:
There was not much more for us to talk about;
Whatever we had once was gone.
So I turned my cab into the driveway,
Past the gate and the fine-trimmed lawns.

Verse 7:
And she said, "We must get together,"
But I knew it'd never be arranged.
Then she handed me twenty dollars for a two-fifty fare;
She said, *(spoken) "Harry, keep the change."*
(To Verse 8:)

TIME OF THE SEASON

Words and Music by
ROD ARGENT

G
and let me try with pleas-ured hands to take you in the
...end Bkgrd.)
cresc.
mf
Em
G
Em
D(9)
C
sun to prom-ised lands, to show you ev-'ry one. It's the time
f
N.C.
Am7
E/B
N.C.
of the sea - son for lov - ing.
2. What's your name?
Bkgrd.: (Clap) (Ah.) (Clap) (Ah.) (Clap) (Ah.) (Clap) (Ah.)

Verses 2, 3, & 4:
N.C.
(4.) (Bkgrd. continues... Who's your dad-dy? Is he rich like me?
(What's your name? Who's your dad-dy? He rich?
3. (Inst. solo ad lib....
Has he tak - en an - y time
Has he tak-en an - y time to
G
to show you what you need to live? Tell it to me
show) ...end Bkgrd.)
cresc.
mf
Em
G
Em
D(9)
C
slow - ly; tell you why, I real - ly want to know. It's the time
f

N.C.
Am7
E/B
1.
N.C.
of the sea - son for lov - ing.
...end solo)
mf
2.
N.C.
Bkgrd.: (Clap) (Ah.__) (Clap) (Ah.__)
p
3.
(Clap) (Ah.__) (Clap) (Ah.__)
4. What's your name?__
mf
Vamp:
Em
C
Em
Repeat ad lib. and fade
(Inst. solo ad lib....

THE TREES

Words by
NEIL PEART

Music by
GEDDY LEE and ALEX LIFESON

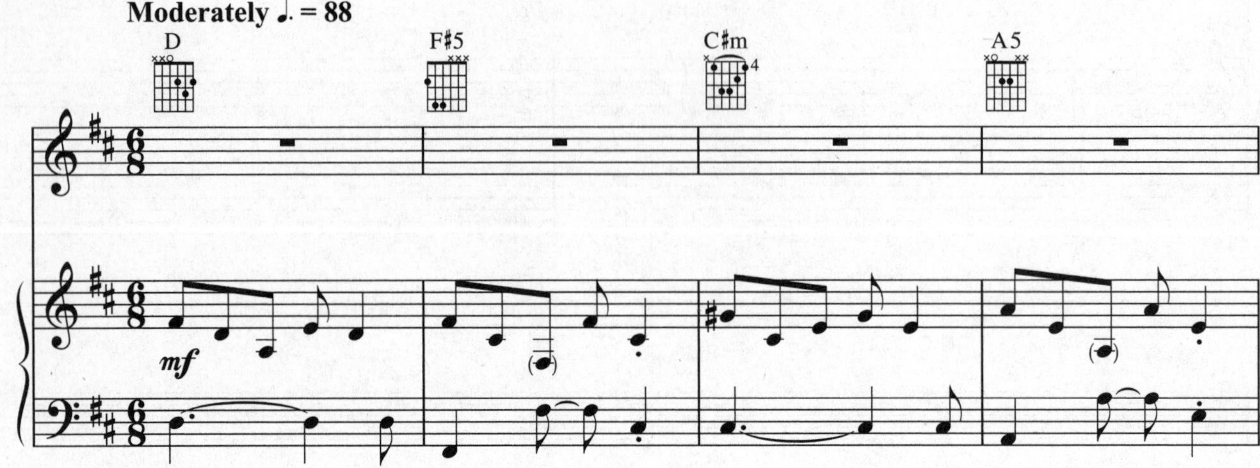

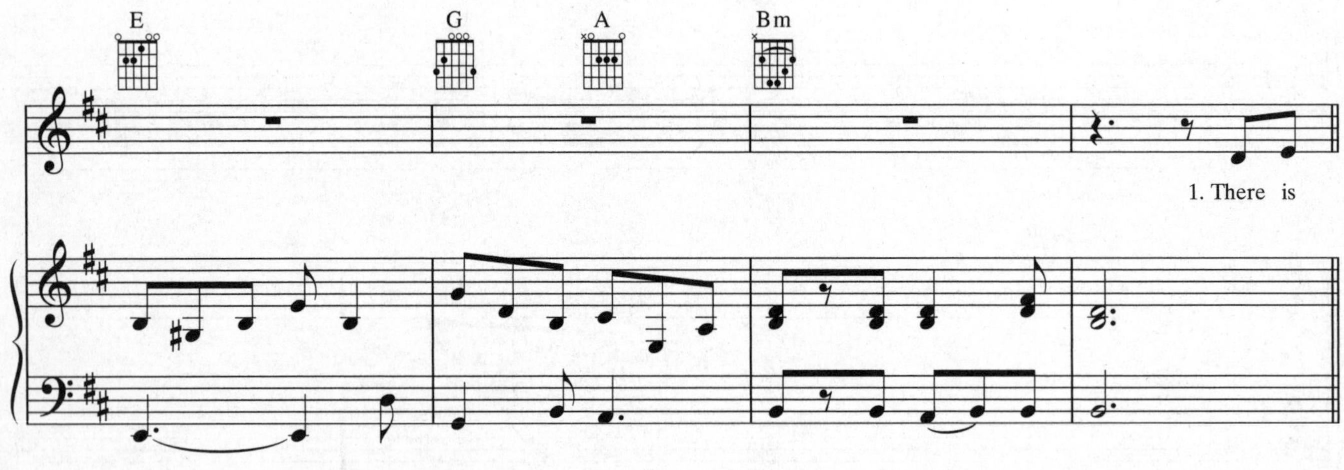

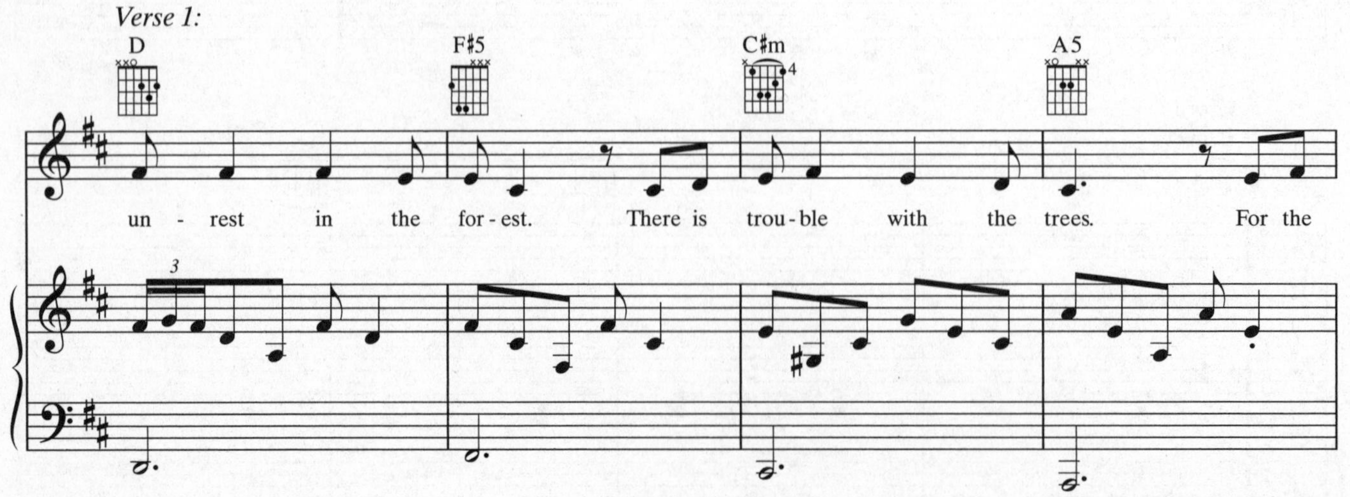

E
G
A
Bm
Ma - ples want more sun - light and the Oaks ig - nore their pleas.
D
F♯5
C♯m
A
E
G
A
Bm
D
A
Bm
Moderately fast rock ♩ = 138
(♫=♪♪)
F♯5
G5
The
f
8vb

A
B
G
D/F♯
trou - ble with the Ma - ples (and they're quite con - vinced they're right,
A/E
A
B
) they say the Oaks are just too loft - y and they
G
D/F♯
A/E
A
grab up all the light. But the Oaks can't help their feel -
B
G
D/F♯
A/E
ings if they like the way they're made. And they
3
3

F♯
G
wonder why the Maples can't be happy in their shade.
Moderately, in 2
(♪=♪)
A
A/G
F♯m7
A/E
There is
D
F♯
C♯m
4
trouble in the forest and the creatures all have fled, as the
E
G
A
Bm
Maples scream "Oppression!" and the Oaks just shake their heads.

D
F♯
C♯m
A
E
G
A
Bm
Interlude:
B5
(Synth.)
A
mp
F♯

A(9)
F♯7sus
D
F
A(9)
E

G/A
G/A
G/B
G/A
G/D
G/A
mf
f
G/B
G/A
G/D
Guitar solo ad lib.
G/A
G/B
G/A

G/D
G/A
G/B
G/A
G/D
(end ad lib. solo)
G
D
A
N.C.
G
D
A
N.C.
G
D
A
N.C.
G
D

A
N.C.
B5
A5
D5
A5
B5
F♯
B5
A5
D5
A5
B5
F♯
So the
A
B
G
D/F♯
Ma-ples formed_ a un - ion and de-mand-ed e - qual_ rights._
A/E
A
B
_ "The Oaks are just too greed - y. We will make_

G
D/F♯
A/E
A
them give us light."
Now, there's no more Oak op-pres-
B
G
D/F♯
A/E
sion, for they passed a no-ble law.
And the
F♯
G
trees are all kept e-qual by hatch-et,
A
axe, and saw.

TOM SAWYER

Words by
PYE DUBOIS and NEIL PEART

Music by
GEDDY LEE and ALEX LIFESON

E
D
Though his mind is not___ for rent, don't put him
No, his mind is not___ for rent to an - y
A7sus
down as ar - ro - gant. His re - serve, a qui - et de - fense,___
god or gov - ern - ment. Al - ways hope - ful, yet dis - con - tent,
C
N.C.
___ rid - ing out the day's___ e - vents: the riv - er.
he knows chang - es aren't per - ma - nent. But change is.
E
D
A7sus

N.C.
What you say__ a-bout his com-pa-ny__ is
And what you say__ a-bout his com-pa-ny__ is
what you say__ a-bout so-ci-e-ty.__ Catch the mist,__
what you say__ a-bout so-ci-e-ty.__ Catch the wit-ness,
catch the myth,__ catch the mys-t'ry, catch the drift.__
catch the wit,__ catch the spir-it, catch the spit.__

A5
B2
B5
A5
The world is, the world__ is. Love and
The world is, the world__ is. Love and
G2
B5
A5
G2
A5
life are deep, may - be as his skies are
life are deep, may - be as his eyes are
E5
To Coda
wide. To -
wide.

day's Tom Saw-yer, he gets high on you,_ and the space he in - vades,_ he gets by_____ on you.
N.C.
(♩ = ♩.)
Guitar solo ad lib.
N.C.

ff
E
D
A7sus
C
D.S. 𝄋 al Coda

Coda
Ex - it the war - ri - or. To - day's Tom Saw - yer, he gets
high on you and the en - er - gy you trade, he gets
right on to the fric - tion of the day.
F♯5
E5
F♯5
Repeat and fade

UNCLE JOHN'S BAND

Words by
ROBERT HUNTER

Music by
JERRY GARCIA

Moderately
G
D
C
D
G
D
mp
C
D
G
Well, the first days — are — the hard-est days; — don't you
buck danc - er's — choice — my friend; — bet - ter
C
G
wor - ry an - y-more. 'Cause — when life — looks like Eas - y Street, there is
take — my — ad-vice. You know — all the rules by now — and the

C
G
Am
Em
dan - ger at ___ your door.
fire ___ from the ice.
Think this through with me; ___
Will you come ___ with me? ___
C
D
C
D
G
Am
Let me know your mind. ___
Won't you come with me? ___
Wo, oh, ___ what I want ___ to know ___
Wo, oh, ___ what I want ___ to know: ___
G
D
G
1.
___ is, ___ are ___ you kind?
___ will ___ you come with me?
It's a
2.
G
C
Am
G
Am
God damn, well I ___ de - clare, ___ have you seen the like? ___

D
C
Their walls are built of can - non - balls; their
G
D
C
D
G
C
mot-to is: "Don't tread on me."
Come hear Un - cle John's Band
mp
Am
G
D
C
play - ing to the tide.
Come with me or go a - lone, he's
G
D
C
D
G
D
C
D
come to take his chil - dren home.
It's

G
C
G
— the same sto - ry the crow told me, — it's the on - ly one — he knows.
I live in a sil - ver mine — and I call it Beg - gar's Tomb.
Like the morn - ing — sun you come — and —
I got — me a vi - o - lin — and I
C
G
Am
like the wind — you go. Ain't no time — to hate, —
beg you call — the tune. An - y - bod - y's choice, —
Em
C
D
bare - ly time — to wait. —
I can hear — your voice. —

C
D
G
Am
G
D
Wo, oh, what I want to know: where does the
Wo, oh, what I want to know: how does the
G
G
C
time go?
song go?
Come hear Un - cle John's Band
Come hear Un - cle John's Band
mp-mf
Am
G
D
C
by the riv - er - side.
play - ing to the tide.
Got some things to talk a - bout -
Come on a - long or go a - lone, he's
1.
2.
G
D
C
D
C
D
here be - side the ris - ing tide.
come to take his chil - dren home.

Dm7
C
Dsus2
C(add D)
Wo, oh, what I want to know: how does the
G
Tacet
song go? Come hear Un - cle John's Band
Drums
by the riv - er - side. Got some things to talk a - bout

G
here be-side the_ ris - ing tide._
Come hear Un-
f
C
Am
G
D
C
cle John's Band_ play-ing to the tide._
Come on a-long or go_
G
D
C
D
Dm7
_a-lone,_he's come to take his chil-dren home._
C
Dm7
C
Dsus2
Da da da da_ da da,
da da da da_ da da.

WEREWOLVES OF LONDON

Words and Music by
WARREN ZEVON, WADDY WACHTEL
and LEROY MARINELL

Moderately ♩ = 108

D C G D C G

mf

Verse 1 (sing 1st time only):

D C G

1. I saw a were - wolf with a Chi - nese men - u in his hand_

Verse 2 (sing 2nd time only):

2. If you hear him howl - ing a-round your kitch - en door,_

sim.

D C G

walk - ing through the streets of_____ So - ho in the rain.

you bet - ter not let him in.____

D
C
G
He was look-ing for a place called Lee Ho Fook's,
Lit-tle old la-dy got mu-ti-lat-ed late last night,
gon-na get a big dish of beef chow mein.
were - wolves of Lon - don a-gain.
Chorus:
A-woo, were - wolves of Lon-don, a - woo!

G
D
C
G
A - woo,
were - wolves of Lon - don,
To Coda
1.
2.
a - woo!
Huh!
Guitar solo ad lib.:
f
3. He's the
…end solo)

Verse 3:
D
C
G
hair - y - head - ed gent who ran a - muck in Kent._
mf
Late - ly he's been o - ver-heard in May - fair.
You bet - ter stay a - way from him. He'll rip your lungs out, Jim.
D.S. 𝄋 al Coda
Huh! I'd like to meet his tai - lor.

Coda

G

Verse 4:

D C

4. Well, I saw Lon Cha - ney walk -

G D C
ing with the Queen, do - ing the were - wolves of Lon - don.
G D C
I saw Lon Cha - ney, Ju - nior
G D C
walk - ing with the Queen, *uh!* do - ing the were - wolves of Lon - don.

G
D
C
I saw a were - wolf drink-ing a pi -
G
D
C
ña co - la - da at Trad - er Vics
and his hair was per - fect.
Chorus:
G
D
C
G
A - woo,
D
C
G
were - wolves of Lon - don.
Huh, draw blood.

D
C
G
A - woo,
were - wolves of Lon-don.
Repeat and fade

WILD HORSES

Words and Music by
MICK JAGGER and KEITH RICHARDS

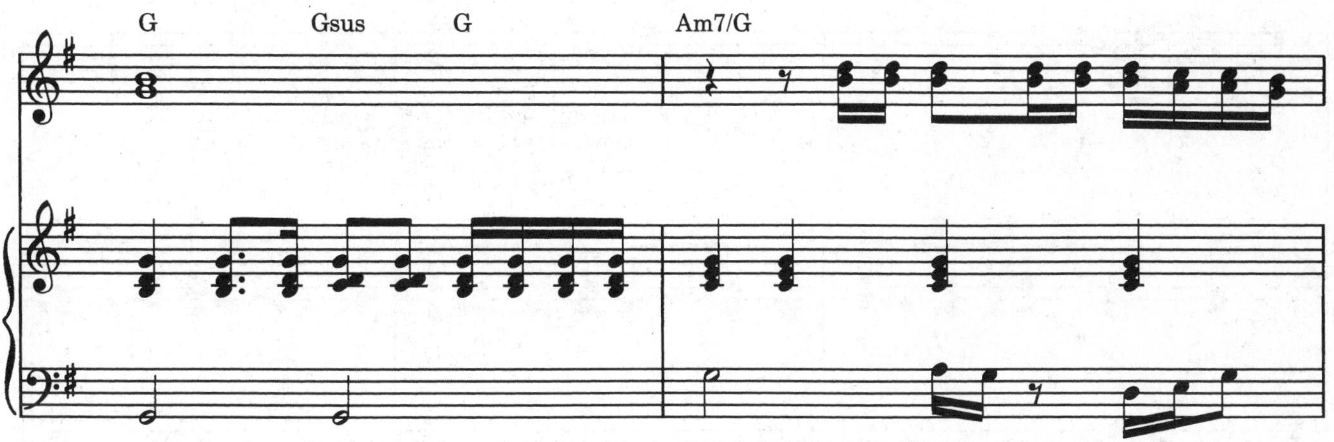

* 8va if played by Guitar.

Bm
G
Gsus
G Gsus
Am
G
is ea - sy to do.
a dull ach-ing pain.
a sin and a lie.
The things you
Now you de -
I have my
C
D
G
Gsus
G
D
D5(2)
D
C(2)
want - ed,
cid - ed
free - dom,
I bought them for you.
to show me the same.
but I don't have much time.
Bm
G
Gsus
G
Bm
Grace - less la - dy,
No sweep-ing ex - its
Faith has been bro - ken,
you know who I
or off-stage
tears must be

G Gsus G Gsus Am G C D
am. You know I can't let you
lines could make me feel bit - ter
cried. Let's do some liv - ing
G Gsus G D D5(2) D
slide through my hands.
or treat you un - kind.
af - ter we die.
Chorus:
Am
Wild
C D D7 G F C Bm
hors - es could-n't drag me a - way.

* 8va if played by Guitar.

* 8va if played by Guitar.

WHEEL IN THE SKY

Words and Music by
NEAL SCHON, ROBERT FLEISCHMAN
and DIANE VALORY

C
B♭
year or more.
I hope she holds on a lit - tle
fore too long.
Ooh, I can't take this ver - y much
Dm
long - er.
long - er, no.
Sent a let - ter on a
I'm stand-in' in the
long sum-mer day made of sil - ver, not of clay.
sleet and rain. Don't think I'm ev - er gon-na make it home a - gain.
C
B♭
Dm
Ooh, I've been run - nin' down this dust - y road.
The morn - in' sun is ris - in', it's kiss-in' the day.

*Sing cues 2nd time.

B♭
Dm
for to - mor-row.
Guitar solo ad lib.:
C2
Dm
C2
Dm
C2
Ahh.
B♭
C
Dm
C
B♭
C

D.S. 𝄋 al Coda
Dm
C
B♭
Oh, the
(end solo)
Coda
G/B
C
B♭
don't know, I don't know, ooo, oh.
Dm
F
C
Oh, the wheel in the sky keeps on turn - in'. Ooo, I
Dm
F
C
Dm
F
don't know where I'll be to - mor - row. Wheel in the sky keeps on

C
Dm
F
C
turn - in'. Ooo, I don't know, I don't know, I don't know.
Dm
F
C
Dm
F
Wheel in the sky keeps on turn - in'. Don't know where I'll be to -
C
Dm
F
C
mor - row. Ooo, the wheel in the sky keeps turn - in'.
Dm
F
Dm
B♭
Repeat and fade
Wheel in the sky keeps on turn - in'.
ff

WHIPPING POST

Words and Music by
GREGG ALLMAN

Moderately fast ♪ = 212

N.C.

mf

𝄋 *Verse:*

A Bm7 C6 Bm7 A Bm7 C6 Bm7

run down. I been lied to, but I

2. *See additional lyrics*

A Bm7 C6 Bm7 A Bm7 C6 Bm7

don't know why I let that mean wom-an make me a fool. She took all my

A Bm7 C6 Bm7 A Bm7 C6 Bm7

mon - ey, wrecked my new car, but

A Bm7 C6 Bm7 A Bm7 C6 Bm7

now she's with one of my good-time bud-dies. They're drink - in' in some cross - town bar. Some-times I

Chorus:
D7
E7
feel, some-times I feel like I been
A7
D7
A7
D7
tied to the whip-ping post, tied to the whip-ping post,
A7
D7
C
Tacet
tied to the whip-ping post. Good Lord, I feel like I'm dy - in'.
N.C.

A
Bm7
C6
Bm7
To Coda
1.
Repeat as needed for solos
2.
Last time D.S. al Coda
2. My friends
Coda
N.C.

cresc.
A
Bm7
ff
C6
Bm7
A
Bm7
C6
Bm7
A
Tacet
Some - times I
D7
E7
feel,
some-times I
feel
like I been

Verse 2:
My friends tell me that I've been such a fool,
And I had to stand by and take it, baby, all for lovin' you.
I drown myself in sorrow, as I look at what you've done,
But nothin' seems to change, the bad times stay the same, and I cannot run.
(To Chorus:)

WHITE ROOM

Words and Music by
JACK BRUCE and PETE BROWN

G/B Bb C D C(9) G/B Bb C
Black - roof coun - try, no gold pave - ments, tired
Plat - form tick - et, rest - less die - sel, good - bye
Con - so - la - tion for the old wound now for -
D C(9) G/B Bb C D C(9)
star - lings. Sil - ver hors - es ran down
win - dows. I walked in - to such a
got - ten. Yel - low ti - gers crouched in
G/B Bb C D C(9) G/B Bb C
moon - beams in your dark eyes. Dawn light
sad time at the sta - tion. As I
jun - gles in her dark eyes. She's just
D C(9) G/B Bb C D C(9)
smiles on you leav - ing my con - tent - ment.
walked out, felt my own need just be - gin - ning.
dress - ing good - bye win - dows, tired star - lings.

G/B
G
C
G
I'll wait in this place where the
I'll wait in the queue when the
I'll sleep in this place with the
B♭
A
C
sun nev - er shines. Wait in this
trains come back. Lie with
lone - ly crowd. Lie in the
G
B♭
C
place where the shad - ows run from them -
you where the shad - ows run from them -
dark where the shad - ows run from them -
1.
D
2.
D
D.C.
selves. 2. You said selves.

3.

D Gm F Dm

selves.

f

C Gm F

Dm C Am7

Repeat ad lib and fade

D C(9) G/B B♭ C

Guitar solo:

YOU CAN LEAVE YOUR HAT ON

Words and Music by
RANDY NEWMAN

E7
(semi-spoken throughout)
Ba-by, take off your coat real slow.
Ba - by, take off your shoes; yeah,
I'll take your shoes.
E13
Ba - by, take off your dress,
yes, yes, yes. You can

E7
E7/G♯
E7/A
leave your hat on.
You can leave your hat on.
(ad lib)
Bm7
E7
You can leave_ your hat on.
sfz
E13
Go on o - ver there,
turn on the light.
No, all the lights.
subito ff
Come back here.
Stand on this chair, that's

E13
right.
Raise your arms up to
the air,
shake 'em.
E7
E7/G♯
E7/A
You give me a rea-son to live.
You give me a rea-son to live.
You give me a rea-son to live.
Bm7
E7
You give me a rea-son to live.

Sus - pi - cious minds are talk - ing,
tryin' to tear us a - part.
They say that my love
is wrong,
they don't know what love is.

They don't know what love is.
mf
f
G5
E7/G♯
They don't know what love is.
They don't
sim.
E7/A
G5
Bm7
know_ what love is.
I know what love is.
sfz
E7
Repeat ad lib. and fade

WISH YOU WERE HERE

Words and Music by
ROGER WATERS and DAVID GILMOUR

Am
G
blue skys from pain.
Can you tell a green field
D/F♯
C
from a cold steel rail?
A smile from a veil?
Am
G
Do you think you can tell?
Did they get you to trade
mf
Verse 2:
C
D
your he - roes for ghosts?
Hot ash - es for trees?

Am
G
Hot air for a cool breeze? Cold com-fort for change?
D/F♯
C
And did you ex-change a walk-on part in the war
Am
G
Em7
for a lead role in a cage?
Dobro solo ad lib.
dim.
mp
G
Em7
G
Em7

A7sus
Em7
A7sus
G
cresc.
Chorus:
C
D
How I wish, how I wish you were here. We're just
mf
Am
G
two lost souls swim-ming in a fish bowl, year af - ter year,
D
C
run-ning o - ver the same old ground. What have we found? The same old

Am
G
fears.
Wish you
were here.
Ending:
Em
G
Em
(2nd time - Dobro doubled by scat vocal cont.)
mp
G
Em
A
Em
A
G
Repeat and fade
(1st time - Dobro doubled by scat vocal)